STEAMY
SEX

Dedication

As always for Nick, my rock

Other books by Dr Pam Spurr

How to be a Happy Human, 10 Essential Principles to Change Your Life

Sizzling Sex, The Doctor's 250 Hottest Tips, Tricks & Techniques

Fabulous Foreplay, The Sex Doctor's Guide to Teasing and Pleasing your Lover

Sensational Sex, The Revolutionary Guide to Sexual Pleasure and Fulfilment

Sex, Guys & Chocolate, Your Essential Guide to Erotic Pleasure

Sinful Sex, The Uninhibited Guide to Erotic Pleasure

The Dating Survival Guide, The Top Ten Tactics for Total Success

The Break-up Survival Kit, Emotional Rescue for Newly Single

Dreams and Sexuality, Understanding your Sexual Dreams

You & Him, Getting to the Heart of your Relationship

Understanding your Child's Dreams

STEAMY
SEX

*The Sex Doctor's Answers
for Keeping it Hot*

DR PAM SPURR

BOOKS

Acknowledgements

Thanks to all of the people who have been completely frank with me over the years when it comes to discussing or writing to me about the most intimate details of their sex lives. Without their stories, questions, dilemmas, worries and suggestions I couldn't have written this book.

Many warm thanks to Jeremy Robson, Lesley Wilson, Ljiljana Baird and Catherine Bailey at JR Books. As always, they've been patient with my idiosyncrasies when it comes to planning and writing a book like this.

For more information about Dr Pam, visit www.drpam.co.uk

First published in Great Britain in 2010 by

JR Books, 10 Greenland Street, London NW1 0ND

www.jrbooks.com

Copyright © 2010 Pam Spurr

A catalogue record for this book is available from the British Library.

ISBN 978-1-907532-24-5

1 3 5 7 9 10 8 6 4 2

Printed by CPI Bookmarque, Croydon, CR0 4TD

Contents

Introduction

I'm continually meeting people who have all sorts of questions they'd like to ask about sex and don't necessarily know who to ask. Or they have worries about their sexual relationship that they can't quite put their finger on – but they know things aren't right. They may not want to go online for answers, knowing that there's so much poor-quality information on the internet. They don't necessarily trust their friends to know the answer, or even feel like telling their friends what they're worried about. It might be something they feel is embarrassing, or at the very least private to their lives.

They've probably heard all sorts of urban myths about sex, and realise they need a trusted source. But they certainly wouldn't go to their GP with a sex question. Neither do they want to go to a sexual health clinic (GUM – genito-urinary medicine clinic), as their dilemma has nothing to do with sexually transmitted infections (STIs) and sexual health generally.

Some of the people who ask in confidence for my advice about a sexual issue – or simply want good, solid and sexy information for improving a stale, predictable sex life – feel quite ashamed or foolish – when they shouldn't. They assume that everyone should know these things, so why don't they? They sometimes feel stupid and naive, and make the completely wrong assumption that everyone else knows everything about sex. Well, 'everyone' doesn't.

As well as those people who want to get some good advice when it comes to sexual dilemmas, issues and difficulties, there are also those people who simply want to know more generally about having great sex and sexual relationships. They may not even be in a relationship but perhaps they think, from past experience, they could definitely do with more knowledge.

This is why I've written *Steamy Sex: The Sex Doctor's Answers for Keeping it Hot,* to show you some simple, usable and often unique solutions to the most asked-about sexual dilemmas. Also as an easy reference guide to top-up your knowledge – in all the main areas – about sex and sexual relationships.

Throughout the book I'll provide you with must-have information for practically every area of your sex life. I illustrate a huge variety of sexual dilemmas with plenty of real-life case studies and answers to the sex questions people ask me. All names have been changed to protect the innocent. Don't skip any passages just because at first glance they don't look like they'll apply to you. Many of the suggestions will apply to various aspects of a sexual relationship – not just the particular dilemma they've been used to help with. At the end of the book I include dozens of websites where you can get products to spice up your sex life or more information.

Time to get started by looking at the very big and crucial area of sexual arousal and desire – and if yours is low, high, mismatched with your partner, or maybe it's disappeared from the face of the earth and you're wondering how to get it back.

Chapter 1

Your arousal, desire and drive

40% of women at any given time lack sexual desire

10% of men at any given time can't get sexually aroused

More than 50% of couples experience mismatched sex drives

These are only three of the many statistics around sexual arousal, desire and drive issues. But I don't necessarily think the statistics are that important. If only one person is worried about not feeling desire, or not getting aroused when they think they should feel aroused, then that one person and their relationship is what counts. Believe me many relationships are in crisis because one or both partners don't feel sexually responsive. Or they may not be in crisis but they certainly aren't flourishing.

Perhaps you've recently looked at your partner – that you love – and wonder why you no longer feel desire for them? Or maybe you find you're still attracted to them but just can't seem to get aroused? Perhaps you're faking it in bed because you just can't get real satisfaction – it's too much stress and too much hassle to try and reach a full climax – but you don't want to hurt their feelings? Or maybe sometimes you feel desire for them, get aroused and enjoy sex, yet other times you don't? These common scenarios – and 1000 other variations – are affecting people like you every day.

Your sexual arousal and desire are such important areas because they form the backdrop to the way you feel about sex – and about yourself, your partner and even with the potential to affect your whole life. As arousal and desire are complicated and cause a lot of confusion, I'm going to give you a straightforward way of thinking about them. Think of your **sexual arousal** as the **physical side** of things – all the changes that go on in your body when you're thinking about sex, looking at something sexy or being touched in a sexy way, etc. The most obvious example is when a man gets an erection – you can see his physical arousal right before your eyes. But that's only one of many changes that happen in a man when aroused, and equally there are many changes that occur in a woman when she is aroused.

Think of your **sexual desire** as the **mental/emotional** side of sex. Your brain starts telling you that you desire someone or something. Your desire can build to such a point that you just have to have sexual release. Or your desire can be interrupted and forgotten about. Of course the biggest 'organ' involved in desire is your brain. It needs to be excited, teased, titillated or stimulated by the sight or thought of someone, or something, to make you feel desire.

When it comes to your sexual drive, I think a helpful way of looking at it is as your over-arching interest in sex, the umbrella over all your feelings, attitudes, your arousal and desire, and need to fulfil these or not. So arousal and desire are one huge package of potential responses – physical and mental – that feed into each other. And your sex drive is the overall total of these things. For instance, let's take a man who loves nice, firm breasts. If he sees a woman wearing a cleavage-revealing top, his brain is stimulated by the image. He literally thinks, 'Wow, she looks desirable.' And then he might even feel some physical response (his arousal) in his loins – perhaps a partial erection.

Or how about the woman who feels desire for her partner when he holds her close in bed at night? Desire fills her heart because she's been rushing around all day, feeling stressed and hasn't had any warm human contact. She feels cared for and enjoys the affectionate way he holds and caresses her. Sex might have been the furthest thing from her mind but just the right touch, the right whisper of 'I love you', stimulates her desire. As this continues, she starts feeling physical arousal too.

These different examples show that sexual desire and arousal can be a brief or potentially long, complicated chain of events. That chain of events can be interrupted at any point, as we shall see in coming questions and case studies. A classic example experienced by many couples is when that moment of bliss they experience as cuddles and affection, turning into foreplay, is interrupted by their baby crying out from its cot – an immediate desire, arousal and passion-killer.

It's recognised across the world that desire and arousal are crucial to enjoying a full sexual experience. And now many in the field recognise 'syndromes' like hypoactive sexual desire disorder (HSDD) – diminished desire – as a big issue for many people. As in the statistic above, some research suggests that this may affect about 40% of women, at some point in their lives.

Desire: check it out

The main reasons why women lose their sexual energy, or desire, are very similar to the reasons men lose their desire. These reasons, or 'sex stressors' as I call them, for both men and women include:

- Lifestyle issues like out-of-control stress and long working hours.

- Lifestyle choices like drinking to excess, smoking, recreational drug use and being overweight that leads to poor circulation – good circulation is important to sexual arousal.

- Emotional problems, such as depression and anxiety.

- Relationship difficulties, a lack of communication, or arguments with their partner that leads to unsatisfactory sex or a complete lack of desire and arousal.

- Certain physical problems like having a bad back, excessive fatigue after childbirth and in the early months of child rearing.

❧ Other surprising things can affect your levels of sexual energy, including medication – typically anti-depressants and blood pressure medications lower sex drive and affect arousal, unrelated worries such as financial problems, and even plain old boredom and routine.

Do any of these sex stressors apply to you, your relationship and/or your life? I'd actually be surprised if at least one didn't.

Lifestyle issues and desire and arousal

In some ways, lifestyle issues are the easiest to identify in dampening down desire and arousal. That doesn't mean that they're easy to solve. But certainly identifying the issue is a good starting point that often gives people the confidence to improve things. Jonathan's experience is a good starting point.

Q **Jonathan: Getting in the mood**

I'm very stressed out and have anxiety problems. This makes getting in the mood really difficult. And sometimes when we start having sex, I lose my focus and we have to stop. My girlfriend wants a better sex life. What can I do to satisfy her and myself?

A You can't treat the symptoms – your and her sexual satisfaction – you have to treat your anxiety problem. I hope you've spoken to your doctor about your anxiety. If not, you need to do so. In the meantime, keep an anxiety diary where you note down the anxious periods during your day. After a week you may find it helps you identify your anxiety peaks.

Most people who suffer from anxiety problems have a distinct pattern. Perhaps you worry most at bedtime, on waking, and towards the end of your day when you worry you haven't finished things. When you've identified your peaks of anxiety, you need to tackle what causes these. For example, do you have anxious thoughts about not finishing your jobs during the day? Try some self-affirmations where you say, e.g., 'why am I worrying? I've achieved lots today. The rest doesn't matter.'

Having got to grips with your anxiety, the symptoms of your anxiety – like the lack of sexual desire – will start to diminish. In the meantime, play a sex game where you pretend to be someone completely different, without a care in the world. You're allowed to feel that way for one hour only. You give yourself permission to shut out anything you worry about. Agree this plan with your girlfriend. By giving yourself permission to let go for that one hour, you may find you shut out the anxieties that you're working to solve. And they become less significant generally once you feel back in control.

Unexpected culprits behind lack of desire

Even when there's an obvious explanation for a lack of desire or arousal, it doesn't mean the answer is straightforward. But when it's an unexpected culprit, people can feel they're fishing around in the dark for a solution. Deborah's story illustrates how things that are seemingly helpful to us (in her case birth control pills) might affect us in unexpected ways.

Q Deborah: Sex drive

Does birth control really affect your sex drive? I am at a point where I just don't want to have sex and it's becoming a problem. I am fine on my 'week off' and then horrible when I am on the pills.

A It varies tremendously between women how much the birth control pill affects their sex drive and desire, and mood. Some women feel absolutely no effect and others experience strong side-effects that completely destroys their desire for sex. As there are so many options available you'd be best advised to go to your healthcare provider and discuss trying another type of birth control pill. You might find a different type doesn't affect your sex drive in this way.

It's crucial to let your husband know that you're concerned over the effect your pill might be having on your desire. You don't want to keep him in the dark about this. Men (and women.) frequently blame themselves for their partner being turned off sex – when there may be another cause, as in your case the pill.

Steamy Sex Tip

Definitely experiment with sex toys – they can really kick start feelings of arousal. Ask him to circle your nipples with a vibrator spending lots of time on them. He can alternate these gentle circles with little kisses and flicks from his tongue. Next ask him to gently trace a line down your stomach to your pubic mound, close your eyes, and enjoy the way the vibrator feels moving slowly across, and around, this area.

If you start feeling in the mood, ask him to lick a couple of his fingers and gently stroke them back and forth across your labia. He should lick them occasionally to keep them super moist as he continues to sexily stimulate your labia.

What happens to your body in that first flush of a relationship?

Let's take a moment to look at the first flush of your relationship, when your body goes into overdrive with a concoction of chemicals. This will give you a small idea of the complexities of your physical reactions during desire and arousal in the early phases of love. It produces extra hormones, as well as other bodily changes. There are even changes in body areas that you might not expect, such as when your lips and the tip of your nose swell just from the slightest touch against his/her skin as they become highly sensitised erogenous zones.

When falling in lust – or even in love – your skin also glows and looks smoother, due to increased hormonal production. And nature's own love potion, the hormone oxytocin, makes you feel good around – and romantically attached to – this new person.

Overall we have a biological 'need' to reproduce with a partner who can help us produce healthy offspring. At a subtle level, much of our attraction is really about us feeling compelled to reproduce – even when at a conscious level we have made the decision not to have children. That decision doesn't stop our body going into sexual chemistry overdrive.

Some of our body chemistry reactions, important to sexual attraction, desire and arousal, and drive include:

- **OXYTOCIN** - the hormone associated with feelings of romantic attachment and sexual attraction.

- **MHCs** - major histo-compatibility complex; molecules associated with a need to mate and select the right partner, in order to produce the best possible and healthy offspring.

- **DOPAMINE** - a neuro-transmitter associated with feeling good.

- **SEROTONIN** - a neuro-transmitter associated with feeling good and well being.

- **ENDORPHINS** - feel-good brain chemicals associated with increased activity - like of the 'bedroom type' in this case.

- **INCREASED BLOOD CIRCULATION** - associated with signs of sexual arousal, like plumping of the lips and a slight swelling to the tip of the nose and a flush in the cheeks.

☙ **BRAIN BLOOD FLOW** - brain scanning techniques have shown that those who feel attracted to someone have certain areas of the brain flooded with blood creating those sensations like butterflies in the stomach, a beating heart and excitement.

A question many couples wonder is why must these lovely feelings calm down eventually? The answer is simple: our bodies *cannot* stay in this heightened state of sexual and romantic arousal longer than a few months as we'd simply burn out. But selfishly, most of us wish this phase could last longer – blast the burnout – we want to stay completely and utterly in lust. That's unrealistic, of course, and if most of us could get past this wish it would help our adjustment back to reality after the honeymoon phase is over.

Apart from burnout, many people don't realise that they can tap into sexual energy that exists within them. Or even prolong the honeymoon phase, or resurrect it from time to time, in a long-term relationship. Some sex therapists theorise that we actually have much untapped energy that can be focused and directed into our sex life. Some believe – as tantric practitioners do – that through meditation and relaxation we can learn to focus our sexual 'chi', or energy. The problem is: *who has much time for meditation and relaxation in our modern lives?* And that's something we all must address – finding a better balance between what we have to do to keep our lives going, and allowing ourselves time to relax to improve our sexual relationship and relationship generally.

Keeping it hot: Desire

If your sexual desire is non-existent, try these tips:

☙ Ensure you're practising 'self-care' - get enough sleep, eat well and rest when needed. This'll give you a good starting point for sorting out your sexual desire.

☙ Get to know your own body. You may lack desire because your partner doesn't know how to turn you on - because you haven't shown him/her what works for you.

◊◊ Get flirty with your lover. We forget how important flirting is to make us *feel good*.

◊◊ Rekindle powerful feelings. You can rekindle your feelings by reminding yourself of why you fell for your partner in the first place.

◊◊ Entice them into more sex by flirting with them on the phone.

◊◊ Get some new sexy things to wear that make you feel good and attractive.

◊◊ Ask what you can do to please your partner. By playing the sex goddess/god you'll have fun, they'll have fun, and you'll get more sex.

◊◊ Start prioritising, and get your working hours in check so you both have enough energy.

◊◊ Get your heart pumping which means that you'll get your all-important circulation going – and you need good circulation for full sexual arousal. All your little blood vessels need to be engorged with blood to fully enjoy sex. Also the pulsating feeling of an increased heart rate mimics the pulsation you get during and after orgasm.

What other surprising sex stressors might affect couples' desire, arousal and drive?

There are many sex stressors that potentially affect a couple's sex life. These include little annoyances that spill into the bedroom, for instance, having argued over what TV programme to watch that evening, or whose parents to visit next weekend. It's important to realise that when you've been irritated by your partner/lover in even these small ways, it stresses your sexual desire.

There are also sex stressors that strike right at the heart of our thoughts about our desirability. A couple of big culprits include believing you've put on weight and are unattractive, or thinking your partner is bored with you. A woman might even worry about putting him off because of the sex 'sounds' she makes as her vaginal muscles have got a bit slack. Or wonder if her selection of nightwear has lost its appeal. And even noticing her partner couldn't take his eyes off the sexy presenter on TV. Equally, a man might get stressed about his expanding waistline or whether he can live up to what his partner reads about in magazines.

Keep It Hot

Always raise such fears and concerns when out of the bedroom, when you're both relaxed, and in a confident tone. If you use a confident tone of voice then your partner will sense it's not such a big deal and you have the confidence to overcome it.

Other sex stressors simply need a practical approach. For instance, get that treasured pet out of the bedroom when you two are feeling in the mood – and who often disturbs you in the middle of things. Fix the lock on the bedroom door so you don't worry your children will interrupt you. Shop for some new sexy clothes together. Allocate a little 'fun time' where you chill-out together and simply enjoy each other's company. Make a promise not to discuss day-to-day problems during your chill-out time. Once you've chilled out, those little stresses and strains will melt away and you'll feel more in the mood for love. Learn to laugh at little things. A lot of couples have a sense of humour malfunction due to the daily grind of life.

What can you do as a couple to overcome 'sex stressors'?

There-are lots of little things you can do to ensure your sex life doesn't get into a rut as a result of a build-up of sex stressors. It's important with little fears about sex – like worrying your partner is bored with you – that you discuss these honestly. It's crucial not to blow them out of proportion and make them into a problem. By talking to your partner you might find they don't even see it as a problem – and that'll help you relax about it.

Steamy Sex Tip

If one of you is stressed over an issue which is putting you off sex, make a joke, tickle them and make them laugh, anything but escalate the issue. Where do you think the saying 'slap and tickle' came from? The fact that it's sexy to laugh and forget your cares.

Having a mismatched sexual desire and/or drive

Having a mismatched sex drive in the bedroom can cause a lot of problems in long-term relationships. David's experience is fairly typical.

Q David: Keeping in synch

Our sex drives seem to be off-schedule. I like to do it at night and she likes to have sex in the morning. How can we get in synch?

A Many men – like you – are nocturnal, i.e., their testosterone peaks at night so they feel more arousal then. Sometimes couples peak together whether morning or night, but many don't. Unfortunately you two have mismatched hormonal patterns, but the good news is you can compromise. Lovemaking should never be just in the morning or just at night as you both will get bored.

Vary your lovemaking by alternating who does the initiating. It's important you're both aware of practical constraints when it comes to compromising. Let's say she wants you to be a 'morning-man'– when it's her turn – but if you often have early work meetings, etc., she should probably try and seduce you on a weekend morning.

Also there are practical ways to stimulate morning desire. For example, would you be tempted by her slipping into a shower – maybe with you – then together returning back to bed for a light, sexy breakfast?

Steamy Sex Tips

You can hand-feed each other toast dripping with honey or jam which of course can be dribbled down your fresh clean bodies to be slowly lapped up.

Why not feed each other luscious fresh strawberries and melon slices...oops one slice dropped between her thighs and then you have to find it.

One way to keep in synch is to get your partner feeling hot at the time they don't normally - but when you do. Become a complete and utter tease to get them in the mood. Cuddle them and then allow your fingers to slip across their hottest erogenous zones - maybe her nipples or pubic mound, or down his thighs and between his legs. Whisper something like, 'I'd love to go down on you right now - I'd give you such pleasure you wouldn't believe it.' Then kiss them again, pull away, and act as if you're going to move off. You might find they pull you back for more.

Kathy's story comes from another side of this particular coin.

Q Kathy: Sex drive

My husband and I have different sex drives, mine being much greater than his. I'm the initiator in the relationship. We both have difficulties in talking about sex. I've half heartedly tried to dress up in sexy lingerie and heels. He responded with a 'What are you doing?' and I felt really stupid. It's starting to take a toll on us and

I'm now sick of initiating. When we do have sex it's very short and only he gets satisfied. What can we do?

A It's quite rare for couples to have exactly the same level of sex drive. Most couples have to make some allowances. But you should be aware that you're not using sex to get affection. Many women do this and actually use sexual initiation when they would be happier with a hug and a kiss. This is discussed in more detail in Chapter 7 on sexual relationship issues.

He needs to check if there's any underlying reason for his low sex drive, for instance one of those listed above such as overwork, drinking too much or the side-effects of medications, etc.

Once you two have talked about these issues in a tactful and loving way then hopefully you'll both gain confidence with each other. Instead of dressing up and surprising him, when you know he's relaxed, ask him what he might like you to do. When you're both in the mood, ensure he doesn't get over stimulated so he doesn't come too quickly. He should be giving you much more foreplay and bringing you to climax, perhaps with a vibrator, before you start penetration. He should also tell you if he's about to climax because he should withdraw before he does. I'll highlight great strategies for slowing him down in Chapter 3.

What if you end up feeling that you're never in 'the mood'?

Many people worry that they've completely lost any sexual desire, for whatever reason, as Jan found.

Q Jan: Losing desire

I feel like I am never in the mood to have sex with my partner anymore. I had already lost desire before we had our baby, and now I'm back at work it's even worse. What should I do? What could be causing it?

A Your biggest sex organ is your brain. There's no way around it – if your brain is stuffed full of worries about work, maybe a sense you're neglecting your husband or being neglected by your husband, worries over when the next baby-gymnastics class is, etc., there'll be no room in it for sexy thoughts. Those issues can and will kill off desire.

You need to prioritise your sex life just as you do, say, meetings at work. If it comes last on the list, you end up with no energy left for it. Give yourself ten minutes per day 'me-time' where you turn off your mobile, your BlackBerry and any other distractions. Lie back and meditate on positive thoughts or read your favourite magazine.

Once every couple of months you should have a full weekend to indulge each other. Share with him your inner fantasies. Many women who lack desire simply aren't telling their husbands what they want. He'll love it if you whisper some sexy thoughts to him or ask him to touch, kiss, etc. you in a new way.

Steamy Sex Tips

Anything that relaxes you is a **great** thing – including enjoying some sexual fantasies and maybe reading a bit of erotica. If you come across a story that really turns you on then describe it to him later on. Also build in proper 'dates' with your husband, as you did earlier in your relationship.

A guaranteed mood enhancer is receiving oral sex without any pressure to make it quick - plus done in a way where it completely spoils you. Slip into some sexy knickers where you can pull the crotch aside to give him access. Ask him to lie back while you crouch over him - slip a pillow under his head to raise it up. Suggest he gently pulls your knickers aside to give him access to give you steamy oral sex.

If you're a super sensitive woman and can't take direct clitoral stimulation, then ask him to kiss and caress you through your silky knickers. He might find it really hot where he can't quite get at the luscious you.

What happens when our partner loses sexual interest?

It's very upsetting when we no longer feel we're desired by our partner. It can derail how you feel about yourself generally. Luckily some take a much more straightforward view as Hannah did. And they simply – as Hannah did – want to help re-stimulate their partner's interest in sex.

Q Hannah: Low libido

How can I psyche my partner back into sex? We've been together five years and apart from this everything is pretty good.

A There are many ways to psyche him up. First re-ignite your flirt-power. We forget to flirt when we've been together a while – just because you're long-term partners doesn't mean you're not supposed to make the other feel desirable. Feeling desirable definitely strengthens feelings of sexual interest, and he may need signals from you that you still desire him. Flirt on the phone, by email and by text message. Phone and remind him of the last time you had hot sex together (sometimes ringing is easier than saying something like this face-to-face).

Steamy Sex Tip

Casually mention you were thinking of buying some new lingerie – describe some sexy bra and knickers set you've seen. Very innocently ask him if he'd like you to model it. Next, be romantic – put on his favourite love songs/mood music. Plan a candle lit picnic on your living room floor if the weather's bad. Stock up with 'rude-food' like oysters, asparagus, avocados, figs, etc., and your favourite little snacks to hand-feed each other. Then bring out your favourite ice cream and chocolate sauce, and turn yourself into a dessert he can feast from.

Have a candlelit bath ready to pamper him in when he gets home. Then slip in beside him. It's the little things that boost the libido. It's when you demand a grand gesture that his libido – and *other things* – will shrink even more.

The uncomfortable feelings we have about our lack of desire

Sometimes we have feelings about our sexual desire that we don't really understand, as in Katy's experience.

 Katy: Sexual attraction

Lately I have been going through this phase where I'm not sexually attracted to my husband. It's frustrating and depressing. The part that is the most frustrating is that I am sexually attracted to other men. We have been married for only seven months now, and I've started to wonder if it's true that seven months is one of those dates where most couples get bored for a little while or is that an old wives' tale? If it's true, what can I do about it? Talk to him or wait it out?

A The seven-month itch is definitely make-believe and I'm not sure who made that one up. However, the seven-year itch has more basis in fact and more recently research shows that there's a 10- or 11-year itch. I'd like to know what's going on with you – are you bored generally in your life? Or is it just with your husband?

If you're bored *generally* with your life, then sit down with him and look at making these three changes:

- Choose one new work-skill to learn and develop, to improve your career and stimulate interest in your life outside your relationship.

- Choose one new hobby or interest to take up with him.

- Plan one exciting getaway together – maybe somewhere you've always wanted to go. By tackling these three areas you should shake up your life enough to actually see it doesn't have to be a boring routine.

If it's boredom with your husband, then choose three ways to shake things up with him. Plan a hot weekend away together, turn off your mobiles, take some new sexy clothes and sex toys, and generally indulge each other. At an everyday level let him know what you'd really like in bed – believe me, men love to be told in detail what they should be doing to you. Don't forget to remind yourself *every day* why you first fell in love with him. Don't lose a good thing so early in a marriage through boredom – that is something you can cure.

Steamy Sex Tip

Surprise him from time to time by dreaming up something a bit wild like meeting him for lunch and go commando (not wearing any knickers).

What if you've never enjoyed a good sexual appetite?

Some people seem to be born with a lower libido, or at least for a great part of their adult lives have a diminished sexual appetite. There can be longer-term medical conditions underlying this or emotional and psychological issues. Peter experienced long-term, low libido.

Q Peter: Sexual appetite

I have never had a healthy sexual appetite. Nowadays, if I am fully aroused, I will eventually want to have sex. However, I see and hear so often how people are 'in the mood' and I never have that feeling naturally. How can I fix this? I don't want my new wife to think she's not good (because she is), it's just my sex drive is stuck in neutral.

A There are many myths around sex that need busting, and one big one is that we all love sex all of the time. Nothing could be further from the truth. People's sex drives vary tremendously and neither a high nor a low drive is better than the other. However, problems start when there's a mismatched sex drive – and the couple are finding it hard to reach a compromise – or when one partner continually lacks sexual desire as you do.

First off, it's terribly important you keep talking and letting her know that she's great in bed, but that you simply have a lower sex drive. Then check out the things that won't help your sex drive as already mentioned, like working too long hours, certain medications, drinking and eating too much, smoking, or depression and anxiety. Through a process of elimination determine how you can change your lifestyle to generally uplift the way you feel. Once you've got rid of any negatives that could be dampening down your desire, ensure you're honest with her about what really turns you on.

It's important you run this past your doctor, too. When someone has experienced lifelong low libido, you need to rule out anything like a long-term medical problem. And never compare yourself to other people and their sex drives – you're an individual with your own needs, including perhaps a much lesser need for sex.

Steamy Sex Tip

Everyone should be honest about what gets them in the mood. But particularly when you have a low sex drive you should feel free to let her know what'll get you hot. Tell her in a soft and loving voice what you'd like to try.

What about feelings of desire towards those outside of your relationship?

Human desire is complicated and wide ranging. We can be deeply in love – and desirous of a partner – but also still feel desire towards others. This isn't necessarily a problem if you understand these feelings of desire and obviously don't act on them unless you are in a non-monogamous relationship. Stephen was experiencing this.

Q Stephen: Laws of attraction

Is it normal to love your partner and enjoy having sex with her, but still desire other women – and want to have sex with them?

A It's absolutely normal to notice and feel attracted to other women (and for women to feel that way about men, other than their partner). It's part of human nature to be drawn to others' physical attractiveness. That said, I never condone taking such interest further. Some people may be tempted to cross the line. That line being: on one side, where a person notices someone that's attractive and fantasises about having sex with them. And then on the other side, there are those that flirt with someone outside of their relationship and get on a slippery slope to infidelity. So it should be a case of 'look but don't touch'.

If you're concerned that you've been finding other women desirable and perhaps flirting with them, then you need to pull back on such behaviour. Don't put yourself in the path of temptation if this is on your mind frequently.

Steamy Sex Tip

Use these feelings and desire for others to liven things up with your wife. Take her away and try the 'strangers in the night' fantasy. This is where you both pretend that you're strangers that have just met and end up having wild sex.

From those with sex stressors to completely sexless couples

Survey reports vary on how many couples have a completely sexless relationship. I think these statistics vary because surveys look at different causes – whether having a sexless relationship is due to desire, arousal and/or sex drive differences, or other issues. Also it's important to recognise that some partners both feel that sex is not an important part of their relationship – and that's absolutely fine as long as they both feel the same way.

I'd like to highlight two main types of sexless couples – where it may or may not be 'fine' for both of them – that I believe are quite common nowadays: dual-income, 'aspirational' couples, and what I'll call 'uninventive' couples.

'Aspirational' couples frequently have great sex lives to start, but are both goal-focused and then go on to conduct their relationship in a non-traditional way. Neither acts as the nurturer, protecting their relationship from an intimacy point of view – something women traditionally did in the past.

They only have time for their goals and aspirations – which is their common bond. Often they end up more as friends and colleagues than lovers sex goes out the window. Many such couples don't care, as long as they get occasional sex before the gym and after checking their work-related emails on a Saturday. They understand each other's aspirational needs and have almost a truce about intimate needs – they won't get in the way.

'Uninventive' couples are those who care about intimacy in their relationship, but get into a sexual routine that's boring. They don't have the creativity or sexual confidence to ensure their sex life doesn't get stale. Sex eventually loses its appeal as it's always 'spoons' on a Sunday morning – very uninspiring.

It's hard to get out of a rut for uninventive couples, or to change the way you run your life for aspirational couples. The crunch usually comes for aspirational couples when one has a crisis and wants the emotional and sexual intimacy that's been missing. Suddenly they want some nurturing – and along with that, sex. As an aspirational couple this means re-prioritising time for each other to be spent nurturing your emotional and sexual intimacy. If you're an uninventive couple it means being willing to take some sexual risks and experiment with new techniques, positions and places.

What about choosing to have a sexless relationship?

Sometimes a relationship can benefit from taking a so-called sex sabbatical. I've been asked fairly frequently about taking these sabbaticals. This is fine if one of you is facing extra demands or a crisis of some sort. Plus you both *discuss* the fact sex will be low on the agenda for a time-limited period.

When it's *not* fine is when you don't communicate over issues that are taking up your time and energy, instead choosing to quietly withdraw from sexual activity. Having to negotiate a sex sabbatical can be a positive thing by developing your abilities to communicate over delicate issues. And you may end up having explosive sex when it's over.

Sex Doctor's Conclusions

I hope this chapter has shown that there are many different ways your sexual desire, arousal and drive can play out in a relationship. Through the variety of questions I'm frequently asked, and I've included, it's quite easy to illustrate that the average couple may face very different challenges and circumstances. But they have one important thing in common – that they can rise to them and use the various solutions and suggestions I've made.

In the next chapter I'll look specifically at issues and dilemmas that women face in their sex lives. But that doesn't let the men off the hook as they're usually directly involved in the solutions, and often in the dilemmas themselves.

Chapter 2

Women's sex questions

At any given time, 70% of women find it difficult to orgasm during penetrative sex

20% of couples now use oral sex to guarantee *her* satisfaction

A number of the issues that affect a woman's sexual response and satisfaction obviously might affect her partner, or equally affect men generally. For instance, her partner's technique may not satisfy her. And that might equally apply to a man and his dissatisfaction with his partner's technique, or even his own private worries about his 'bedroom skills'.

This is why I'm separating questions about issues concerning sexual technique – that frequently apply to both men and women – into Chapter 5, from things that more specifically apply to women. Or at least the things that women worry about, complain or ask about. In the next chapter I'll do the same, tackling issues more specifically applying to men and their sexual satisfaction.

The big Oh-oh-heaven

Let's begin with the big 'O' – orgasms. There's been so much written and said about the female orgasm that I'm going to select some of the most commonly asked questions and issues to highlight for you. Something very common is women wondering what sort of 'problem' they have when they can't orgasm. Chloe puts it succinctly.

Q Chloe: The big O

If you don't have orgasms, is it automatically an emotional issue? In other words, are there physical causes for a lack of orgasms as well?

A Physical causes for anorgasmia – where a woman regularly can't reach orgasm despite adequate sexual stimulation – are fairly rare. Actual nerve or other damage is only found in a minority of women – usually due to trauma to the genital region, complications from genital surgery or diabetic neuropathy, and other such causes.

However, many emotional and psychological issues are at play that affect a woman's chances of reaching orgasm. These include:

- Feelings of inhibition, shyness, low self-esteem and body image difficulties.

- Relationship–interpersonal issues such as arguments and unhappiness with her partner, or a partner with poor technique.

- Mental health issues like depression and anxiety.

- Let's not forget lifestyle choices: excessive alcohol, drug use, smoking and high-stress will adversely affect arousal.

- There are things that affect orgasm, besides medical problems, such as medication side-effects as noted in the last chapter, which may affect desire and arousal. Think of the chain reactions between desire, arousal and then onto a full climax. You already know how desire and arousal can be affected, and reaching orgasm can be affected by the same things.

The first step is always to go through these potential factors to see which apply to your life. Ruling out any medical issues, try and tease out the various things you think about before and during sex.

It's crucial to be honest with your partner about which of these factors might apply to you. Always put these across in a positive and confident way so that your partner doesn't feel threatened. Using a 'pointing-the-finger-of-blame' technique is unlikely to help, and very likely to hinder, progress with these things. I offer loads of practical and do-able advice about communication techniques in Chapter 4.

The things we women wonder about our sexual response

Many women try to arm themselves with information by reading magazine articles, books and searching the internet about orgasms. That's because so many women find it hard to reach climax. But sometimes these searches lead to even more questions, as Kelly found.

Q Kelly: The best orgasms

I bought a magazine with an article about 'getting the best possible orgasms' and felt quite confused by some of the information. Are there really two types of female orgasm (clitoral and vaginal), or is it all the same thing?

A It's very rare that women can orgasm *without* clitoral stimulation of some type. Most are highly reliant on adequate clitoral stimulation. A few (and rare) highly orgasmic women can orgasm through stimulation of their breasts, buttocks and vagina alone. As the vaginal barrel contracts during orgasm, many women identify these vaginal sensations as their 'orgasm'. It is easy to do, particularly as these sensations are often clearly identifiable amongst the other highly dispersed sensations of clitoral arousal and changes, pelvic floor sensations, and vaginal changes during orgasm.

If you're achieving orgasm it can be interesting, but not necessary, to try and identify where your most powerful sensations come from. But this can potentially interrupt your orgasmic flow, so don't get hung up on it.

Sometimes our bodies work in strange ways and even if we start out highly aroused with our partner, women can often lose the 'moment'. Some very sensitive women find *any* distraction to their arousal kills off any chance of reaching climax, unless they start all over again. And sometimes women are too tired to start all over again. It's always crucial to think about creating a sensual environment that prevents distractions. For example, things like whether you might get 'new-baby-interruptus' to your lovemaking – where a new mother is highly sensitised to even the smallest noise their baby makes. In this case, unless you have an ill infant, you're allowed to turn off the baby monitor for 15 minutes of pleasure.

 Steamy Sex Tip

Ask him to do the 'V' for Victory technique – placing his index and third fingers either side of your clitoris, pointing downwards towards your bottom, arching over your pubic mound. He holds this finger position and gently and sensually moves his fingers a tiny bit up and down repetitively. This is guaranteed to arouse any woman.

And there are times when we wonder about the way our bodies work, as Becky did.

Q Becky: Arousal

Can a woman be physically aroused and not realise it? I was daydreaming once about something unrelated to sex and then found myself feeling slightly aroused and was very surprised by this.

A Yes, in a number of day-to-day activities a woman can become sexually aroused at a sometimes barely perceptible level. It can happen in the presence of a powerful (power is an aphrodisiac after all.) or attractive person when small elements of arousal occur. Or, say, when engrossed in a film or a book with an erotic or romantic theme and a woman becomes aroused at a subconscious level. Of course at other times she'll know full well she's been aroused by a film scene or attractive person.

At other times it seems like there isn't any connection between something like a daydream – that isn't about anything erotic – and finding yourself semi-aroused. The simple act of relaxation – which we do when we daydream – can allow impulses and urges to escape from our subconscious mind.

Finding yourself aroused or feeling desire can help 'prime' you for a sexual encounter, and it's good to be in touch with such feelings. Any heightened awareness of your sexuality will increase positive feelings of self-belief about your sexiness. Let me repeat myself on an important message, for women, particularly: sex is in the mind – the mind being the biggest sex organ – so positive feelings are beneficial.

Don't buy into the myths around orgasm

I find there's a lot of bad information given out particularly in women's magazines – even some of the more respected ones (that I've sometimes written for.). Sometimes there are wild claims like the best orgasm you'll ever have is when you have a 'mutual orgasm'. If something seems wildly 'aspirational', or makes you feel like you have to be an Olympic athlete in the sport of sexual pursuits, then ignore it. Otherwise, if you're like Sam you may find you start feeling bad about your sex life for no reason whatsoever.

Q Sam: Sexual connection

Is mutual orgasm the ultimate sign that you're connecting sexually with your partner – true or false? And why? I love my long-term boyfriend very much but this has never happened to us, and it made me feel that we were missing out.

A One of the biggest – and sometimes most damaging – orgasm myths (after the myth that there's something wrong with you if you don't orgasm during penetration) is that the gold standard of pleasure we should aim for is climaxing *together*. Let me reassure you that it's very rare for couples to manage this and they shouldn't feel the pressure to try. Instead couples should be encouraged to relax and enjoy finding out what works for her (e.g. any combination of manual, oral, and/or penetrative sex plus the use of sex toys) as well as ensuring he then is satisfied.

The biggest problem in buying into the mutual-orgasm-is-best myth is that you start focusing too much on where your partner is – and how near they are to orgasm – and can miss the moment yourself. What's important is that a man always ensures that his partner has reached climax before he reaches his – as climaxing before her can leave her high and dry, when he loses his erection.

As a couple you should never feel that you must go on and on, if for some reason either person isn't stimulated enough, isn't in the mood, has lost their moment or just simply isn't going to have a climax during this particular sex session. There's nothing wrong about sometimes enjoying sex play that doesn't end in orgasm.

One myth that's thankfully less and less prominent is that a woman's 'abnormal' if she can't orgasm when a man's inside her during penetrative sex. And for some women they find they can only orgasm through masturbation. Amanda worried about this.

Q Amanda: Faking it

I'm 30 and I've never had an orgasm during penile penetration, oral sex or any kind of foreplay with a sexual partner. I'm only able to get an orgasm by a specific way I masturbate (on my stomach with a pillow). I've tried many different sexual positions but nothing has ever come close to this sensation. I've been faking orgasms with my fiancé for four years now and I can't ever tell him the truth. I know it would break his heart. How should I handle this?

A It's time to stop faking. And it is crucial in a committed relationship (and even in a casual fling) that you can bring up any bedroom issues like this. Some women find it impossible to confess that they've been faking and instead use the following tactic. If you can't face him honestly with this then say something like you've 'been a bit stressed recently and are finding it hard to get aroused, so can you try a new form of stimulation'. This tactic is a halfway house that can start real communication. Then guide him into recreating the stimulation you get through masturbation.

Many women feel exactly as you do, and only get adequate stimulation by using something like a pillow because they haven't been honest with their partner.

If you two enjoy using sex toys during your sex play, there are now various vibrators with a 'flattened' shape (almost like the palm of the hand) that gives great stimulation to women who like the sensations you do.

Steamy Sex Tip

You can make guiding him part of a fantasy role-play where, say, you pretend to be the 'patient' and he's the 'doctor' and you guide him in his examination. Take it slowly, one step at a time, and hopefully you can recreate those sensations with him.

For some women, only 'oral' will do

Ellen was happy about only being able to orgasm through oral sex, but it was her boyfriend who was concerned that the only way she ever achieved satisfaction was through oral sex. Again, I'd like to reassure anyone – and their partner – that whatever works for you is always great.

Q Ellen: Oral only

I don't orgasm during sex, which, I should point out is fine by me. Because my boyfriend enjoys giving me oral sex and I can orgasm that way, I didn't think it was a problem. But funnily enough my boyfriend disagrees. Apparently he feels responsible that it's his fault if I don't climax. While I don't physically enjoy sex, I emotionally enjoy it when he orgasms and would be satisfied with just that, but I don't know what to do about his feelings. It's become a problem because after we have sex he gets emotionally withdrawn and makes negative comments about our sex life. Then I feel bad and it ends up making us not want to try again.

A You're experiencing what about 70% of women do to one degree or another – the fact that they're unlikely to orgasm through penetrative sex. But for many of those, like you, they can do through oral sex. Obviously with such a percentage this is not unusual and you are not alone. The reason why so many women successfully climax through oral sex is due to the fact that it's easier to achieve the 'right' amount of pressure and stimulation that they need to bring them to climax. So the fact they can enjoy climaxing this way rather than through penetration is frequently because they haven't managed to learn how to get the right friction and stimulation through penetrative sex.

You're not alone, as many women who climax better through oral sex have to face their partner's disappointment that he can't give them orgasms regularly through penetration. Or they have to face their partner's questioning them about whether previous partners have given them orgasms through penetration.

The fact that your partner gets withdrawn over this is his hang up. Where this stems from is the fact that he feels completely responsible for your sexual enjoyment. That means he wants you to enjoy sex the way he thinks you should. And his thinking is that it should be through penetration – and that you'd probably have the best orgasms that way. But you don't.

So where does this leave you and couples in this position? With the 'C' word – you need to communicate better. So that he understands that your sexual enjoyment (just like his) is a mutual responsibility. And that sexual enjoyment shouldn't be about one way of climaxing being better than another.

It's a good idea to let such partners have the statistics that many women find it hard to reach orgasm during penetrative sex. Emphasise that everyone needs a different rhythm – so a man and woman may not be able to get the same excitement from the same sex position. And often what position works for a man doesn't give her the clitoral region stimulation against his pubic bone that many women need for climax.

 Steamy Sex Tip

It shouldn't matter whether you climax through oral sex, penetrative sex, manual sex or a vibrator, as long as you both believe that sexual pleasure is important and you don't have to reach climax by one set route.

Try the CAT position – the clitoral alignment technique. This is where you are on top of him, 'shimmied' up an inch or two, with your clitoral region against his pubic bone. Guide how you move so that you can maintain good clitoral stimulation. You should agree that you dictate for how long – and in what way – penetration occurs. It's almost as if you're masturbating against his pubic region.

Some women wonder, as Zoe did, about whether there's an emotional reason why they don't climax during full sex.

Q Zoe: Elusive orgasms

I orgasm fairly easily during masturbation and oral sex with my husband, but I have never been able to have one during penetration. Is this a physical thing or a mental thing?

A As we now know this is incredibly common. And it's important to consider if it's a physical 'thing', a mental 'thing', or a combination of both. Let me explain.

Physically a woman needs the right type of physical stimulation (for her.) to reach full orgasm. Some types of stimulation will sexually arouse her but won't be quite right to lead to actual climax. This means her clitoral region might not be stimulated against a part of her partner that gives her the right stimulation.

It can be a mental thing where a woman simply finds it hard to 'let go' during full penetrative sex. She may have some emotional and/or sexual inhibitions that stop her reaching climax, even though physically she's able to. And of course it can be a combination of the lack of the right physical stimulation for her and some emotional inhibitions.

What you need to do is think through these possibilities and how they apply to you. For instance, if you lack trust with your husband or feel silly letting go in the middle of sex, or feel shy and inhibited, you need to sort out the reasons for this and how you can solve it. Building trust and confidence between you – and confidence of your own that you deserve to enjoy a full sexual relationship – is the best starting point. The communication techniques in Chapter 4 will definitely help.

On the physical side, your husband manages to give you exactly the right friction and pressure you need during oral sex to make you climax. And when you masturbate you also know exactly what pressure, speed, friction, etc., works to bring yourself to orgasm. You need to take this knowledge into penetrative sex and alter the position you two use or try completely new positions (like CAT just mentioned). Or maybe you could introduce your hand, or his hand, to your clitoral region while you're having penetrative sex. With this added manual stimulation it may bring you to climax.

Let your husband know you want to sex-periment – suggest this in a positive and upbeat way to make it sound like fun rather than difficult or troubling.

Steamy Sex Tip

Alternatively you might slip a vibrator between you, giving you clitoral pleasure, while you continue to have penetrative sex.

Some orgasm facts

Here are a few interesting facts about orgasms:

- The male ejaculation has been measured at 42 miles per hour on orgasm.

- Forget an 'apple a day' – an orgasm a day will keep the doc away, with it boosting the body's lymphocytes, important for a healthy immune system.

- Orgasms actually relieve headaches by releasing the tension constricting blood vessels in the brain.

- Orgasms are good for mild depression as they facilitate release of endorphins – the brain's natural feel-good chemicals.

🔥 During orgasm (and general sexual arousal) the tip of your nose swells as well as your buttocks.

🔥 One survey found 70% of women had faked orgasm at some point. I'm not surprised in the slightest by this.

🔥 No two orgasms are alike, even within the same person.

An important point to make is to never compare your orgasms to a friend's. Women are often happy to discuss the details of their sex lives with friends (in a way that most men would never) but that means they're much more likely to make unhelpful comparisons. Susie wondered about her orgasms compared to friends.

Q Susie: What is an orgasm?

There seems to be a popular notion of orgasms as a toe-tingling, earth-shaking event. Is it always that way? Can a woman have one and it be so mild it barely registers on her Richter scale – or even so mild she doesn't realise it happened? My best friend seems to have a completely different experience.

A Never, ever compare yourself to a friend. Yes, it can be fantastic talking to a girlfriend about the intimate details of your sex lives. But it should never be about thinking there's something wrong with you or that your sex life doesn't live up to hers. Even within a single person no two orgasms are alike. Sometimes they're more powerful and sometimes they're incredibly gentle.

One indication that you've had an orgasm is the sense of release from sexual tension. Even a gentle one can give you that sense of release. If yours are so gentle that you don't feel that release or a sense of letting go physically, then perhaps you've got near to orgasm but not all the way. There is lots of information about sexual technique in Chapter 5 that may help you.

Men, too, wonder about the different ways their previous and current partners respond sexually. Jack made a classic comparison between two of his lovers.

Q Jack: How does she feel?

My wife seems to have very different orgasms to my ex-wife. My ex-wife used to literally claw at the mattress as she climaxed. She made a lot of noise and it was obvious when she had an orgasm. But my new wife barely makes a sound except a few gasps. Does this mean it doesn't feel as good for her?

A There's no right or wrong way to experience an orgasm.

Women experience orgasms very differently both in how they feel it and the actual physical changes that occur in their body as measured in research by sexologists. They also differ in the way they express it – anything from quiet moans to loud screams. Not only will two different women describe their experiences differently, but a woman herself will notice that sometimes they are powerful and rhythmic building to a crescendo, other times gentle, and sometimes a short, sharp shock.

Steamy Sex Tip

Ask your wife if there's anything else you can do to satisfy her. And let her know it's okay to make noise when she climaxes. Some women (and some men) worry about making too much noise, when in reality they'd like to let rip with some.

Sometimes it's all about the timing

Many women do get the right stimulation from their partner – whether through penetrative, oral or manual sex. However, it's the timing that's a problem for some women, as Rachel has found.

Q Rachel: A long time coming

It takes me a very long time to climax. Normally, we'll be 30 minutes into sex and I may or may not have had an orgasm. My boyfriend is my first and he says that this is an unusually long time. Is there anything I can do to help speed up the process?

A This is definitely NOT an unusually long time. The average

woman (and none of us are average, are we?) takes around 25–30 minutes of foreplay, stimulation and/or penetration to reach climax. Of course there's wide variation but what really counts is when two unique people come together as a couple that they enjoy what they're doing. It's important not to worry about the time others spend on sex.

Some women find that the time it takes them to get sexually aroused and climax speeds up with a couple of important factors. First, that they feel loved and romanced. There's hardly anything that'll make you feel sexier than feeling wanted, loved and desirable. Discuss with your boyfriend having a little more romance and creating a generally loving atmosphere between you two.

The second big factor is that women tend to climax more quickly when they feel completely free and confident about saying exactly what stimulation turns them on. For example, maybe he gives you some pleasure during foreplay but tends to lose the rhythm, speed and/or friction you like. This means the build-up to your climax is interrupted. Gradually introduce some really sexy detail about what he does that really gets you going. It's important to return the favour to him and ask him if he can tell you exactly what he likes. If you two can communicate over these couple of important areas then you might find things speed up, but they may not: some women simply take longer and that's no big thing.

Steamy Sex Tip

Don't be frightened to say to him, 'that's perfect, stay there', when he hits the right spot. In fact, tell him ahead of time that you're going to let him know when he's doing everything just right.

Pregnancy, babies and sexual feelings and experiences

I've mentioned feelings in terms of feeling inhibited and confident to say what you want. But what happens when our lives – including our sex lives – change particularly during something as important as pregnancy? Thomas was concerned about how pregnancy affected his wife.

 Thomas: Sex during pregnancy

When my wife became pregnant, she suddenly didn't want to be touched or have sex. (We had a great sex life before the pregnancy.) We got cuddly once in this time but we stopped as she said she wasn't in the mood. I understand that she is going through changes, but I can't help but take this personally – like she just doesn't want to have sex with me and I don't know why. Please don't misunderstand me as I'm very happy we're having a child, but I was wondering if many women feel this way? Also, do you think her sexual mood may change, or is there a chance we might not have sex until after the baby is born?

A There are a number of important things here. There's a difference between her simply not being in the mood or if she experiences discomfort when you've tried having sex due to the changes in her body. If she experiences discomfort, then a little gentle and careful experimentation might find a position and technique that works for her. If she's not in the mood then it may be her hormones are dictating these mood changes. And she might simply be tired. If that's the case, be extra helpful with chores and errands, and making sure she rests. Not only is that kind and loving, but she may recover some of her libido.

It could be other things, though. Some women fear that having sex during pregnancy might hurt their unborn child in some way, despite reassurance from their healthcare professional. Or she might feel her role is now different as an expectant mother. If she has any fears about sex during pregnancy, then offer to go along to her healthcare provider and encourage her to ask any questions she wants answering. Unless she has some sort of complication with her pregnancy, sex will not hurt your unborn child.

It's a little trickier if she sees her role as expectant mother and no longer as your lover at this point. Such beliefs can be deeply ingrained. If you explore them and emphasise how you see her as a multi-faceted person, that'll help.

Any of these things can change throughout a pregnancy. Keep communication lines open with her about being intimate. Be romantic and loving with her. Let her know you're not always trying to get her to have sex when you give her a cuddle. The more she trusts you to try and understand how she's feeling, the more likely she'll open up and hopefully start to enjoy sex.

Although both parents-to-be might be excited about the baby's arrival, for one reason or another they may not be excited by sex during pregnancy. If not handled with utter tact and in a loving way, such feelings can really hurt the other partner.

Liz and then Sasha are having very different experiences that affect their and their partners' feelings.

Q Liz: Low sex drive during pregnancy

I'm six months' pregnant and have a completely out of whack sex drive. As soon as my husband and I start signalling to each other about cuddling up and having sex, I get really self-conscious and don't want him to touch me because of the weight that I've gained. He is fantastic and tries to make me feel sexy – which makes him all the more amazing – but as soon as he touches me I want to hide under the covers. What can I do to get our sex life back where it was before I gained the weight?

A

Liz's question perfectly illustrates the 'I think I'm fat, so he'll think I'm fat, too' complex. We women are particularly guilty of this. We get completely wrapped up in our own little insecurities – no matter what form they take – and then we assume our partners think the same. Let me assure you that rarely does a man think in the same critical way about your body that you do.

Once we can get our insecure heads around this fact, it's easier to relax and accept such sexual attention. Thankfully the majority of men see an overall picture of the woman they love. They don't notice any little excess weight here, a little bulge there. Instead men are likely to admire the whole package without the detail.

Research proves men see things differently – and you can do a simple test at home to prove this point to yourself. Ask your husband to find, e.g., the mayonnaise in the fridge. I bet he takes far longer than you would take to find something in the fridge. This is because they see the *whole* fridge and *not the detail* of the little items in it. Remember this.

With that thought in mind, please believe that he wants to touch and hold you. Talk yourself up each and every day. Remind yourself what a fabulous mother-to-be you are and how you should be kinder to yourself. Next, start taking gentle exercise each and every day. Resist jumping in the car, and walk to places instead.

Don't use the lift or escalator, walk upstairs. Even when doing chores around the house, put some elbow grease into them and burn off some calories. It's important to be fit and well, but not be obsessed about your weight.

Q Sasha: Sexual attraction during pregnancy

I'm currently seven and a half months' pregnant, and my husband and I have been very open and communicative about our needs and desires. He has told me that honestly he simply isn't attracted to my 'tummy' (he's already stated that he's not afraid of hurting the baby, etc.). This hurts to hear, but I also prefer his honesty. So my question is, I still have needs/desires and feel that as everything else in our relationship is about compromise, so this should be about compromise. And no matter how his desire has decreased due to my growing tummy, that he should still make an effort, of which I see none. Am I wrong to expect this? Also, I was wondering, on average how often do married couples with kids have sex?

A Let's get this important issue straight. In the ideal world there should always be compromise in the bedroom, just as a couple should compromise in every other aspect of a relationship. However, every couple lives in the real world and compromise isn't always the solution. This is a temporary situation, with only six weeks left to go until your baby arrives. To force the issue of him not finding your pregnant tummy 'attractive' and still insist he ensures your needs are met, could be very damaging to your relationship.

No one should be forced into sexual activity that actually turns them off. He obviously desires you apart from this. Everyone has their own little likes and dislikes. But when it comes to sex, compromising on the dislikes can become such a turn off that the person is turned off sex generally within the whole relationship. That is never helpful.

Therefore in this particular situation a woman shouldn't demand that her partner make love to her. However, a possible solution is to sound the 'squeamish' man out about fondling you with his hands (manual stimulation) or using a vibrator to stimulate you to orgasm.

When it comes to how much sex couples have after having children, it dramatically decreases in the first year for the majority of couples. However, after the first year many couples find they can rebuild a satisfying sex life if they communicate their feelings and compromise with each other.

Perhaps your needs for sexual release in the last six to eight weeks of pregnancy, in this type of case, should be met through self-pleasure – masturbation. There's nothing wrong with masturbation, whether pregnant or not.

Post baby sex concerns

After the birth of a child there are many things that come into play affecting a couple's sex life. Amanda experienced what many women experience in the first six to nine months after childbirth. And something that's important for new dads to recognise.

Q Amanda: Post-baby sex

I have read in so many books and magazines about how to get back into a sexual relationship with your husband after having a baby, but nothing really seems to get me in the mood. It seems like my mind wanders during sex and I can't focus on feeling good. What can I do?

A This is a perfect description of what many new mums, and some new dads, experience. They've been so overwhelmed with the endless baby chores during the day that their minds simply can't focus. If you can't even focus on the last paragraph you read in your novel, or the last thing said in a television drama, you're hardly likely to focus on any sexual feelings.

To begin with, I'd like any new mum who's feeling worried, lacks energy and enthusiasm, and/or is feeling down, to ask your healthcare professional about post-natal depression, because in mild cases the main symptoms can be a lack of focus and loss of sex drive.

Steamy Sex Tips

Next, if your mind's going to wander, let it wander to a fantastic fantasy that turns you on. You can then give a little delicious detail about it to your husband. By discussing a highly erotic fantasy story-line, you may find you relax back into the moment.

Another top tip is definitely get someone you trust to baby sit, so you two can simply enjoy a little quality time on your own.

Don't talk about the 'baby things', but instead talk about the things you two enjoy. It doesn't have to be a time where you have sex, it's simply to go for a walk or watch a romantic DVD together. Whatever you do, don't hide this from your husband. Let him know how much you love him but are perhaps a bit mentally or emotionally overwhelmed by all the changes a baby brings.

After a couple's had a baby, men can feel left out in so many ways. Because of these feelings they can quietly start worrying about their relationship generally and the sexual side of things specifically. Jack put this succinctly in a question.

Q Jack: Post-baby desire

I worry about the way my wife feels about sex now that we've had a baby. Can you please give me some pointers of what to expect.

A The demands of new motherhood along with hormonal changes mean that many women go right off sex – just the idea of it can send some running for household jobs like the ironing to avoid it. As well as adopting an entirely new routine that leaves them little time for themselves, many women get 'cuddled-out' where they've been holding their baby on and off all day and actually don't want any physical contact for a time in the evening.

Men take this as an immediate rejection, so it's important to explore this with your partner – and this comes down to good basic communication. Add to this the fact that women experience a number of physical changes to their figures, and their confidence can plummet with the thought of getting intimate with their partner. Often the men feel very differently towards their partners after childbirth. They'll feel there's something special about their partner as the 'mother of their child'. This means that emotionally a man might find it hard to reconcile her role as a new mother with her still being a sexual woman.

We often forget that men can also feel stressed and tired by the new routine, but are worried to talk about their feelings for fear of being misunderstood. Such factors mean many couples get their wires crossed – and either partner may end up feeling rejected.

So these are all important things to consider and be open about.

Steamy Sex Tip

As long as you know she's not exhausted, why not make tonight different? After a quick catch up on both of your days, cut out any passion-killing talk about babies. Then go for some easy and sensual techniques like the 'Figure of 8 Massage'. Dim the lights, light a few candles, put on some soothing music and ask her to lie on her back. You can start at her neckline with your well-lubricated finger tips and curve around the outside of her breasts with both hands, meeting at her tummy button. Then curving out again around her pelvis and meeting at her inner thighs. If you do this gently it'll feel heavenly, and awaken her erogenous zones.

Physical discomforts during sex

Discomfort during sex – for whatever reason, medical or emotional – can be very distressing for women. Obviously if she's distressed it affects how he feels about the sexual side of things too. Carol was experiencing something that many women do – where their 'thinking and feeling' doesn't match up to their 'physical' experience during sex.

 Carol: Discomfort during sex

I love my husband and definitely have the emotions and feelings that make me want to have sex with him. I also love foreplay and some of the things he does feel really nice and pleasurable. But frequently I'm uncomfortable during sex. Sometimes I'd describe it as almost being more in pain, more than experiencing pleasure. What's wrong with me or with my body?

 There are many reasons why women experience pain on/ during/around intercourse. Some reasons have an emotional basis and others can have a physical cause. The great starting point you have is that you love your husband and foreplay with him. The fact that you find some things pleasurable is a big positive.

I have a doctorate in psychology, not medicine, but I do know it's important to rule out any medical/physical causes like perhaps an ongoing infection. It's important to get this checked out by your healthcare provider or sexual health clinic in order to rule it out – or treat any such cause. Don't worry as this is done in confidence and with people who know about sexual health.

On the emotional side, it'd be very helpful if you thought through whether or not there's a pattern to the discomfort you feel? For example, do you have periods of high stress in your job or some other aspect of your life? When in a state of stress all of our body gets tense and that includes a woman's vaginal muscles. As soon as these tense up sex can become painful.

Or could it be that there's something you feel guilty about during sex? Perhaps there is part of you that feels you don't deserve to have great sex or that somehow sex is 'dirty', so if you enjoy it then you must be 'dirty'. Many people have sexual inhibitions or feelings that what they're doing isn't 'right' because of attitudes handed down from their parents' generation.

Thinking about these things is likely to help you identify where this pain comes from. It's important to share these things with your husband so that together you can both make sure you enjoy your sexual relationship.

If you decide it might be something to do with your emotional feelings – I'm sure your partner would like to be made aware of your feelings. Because if you're feeling a little insecure, tense or inhibited, together you can talk about the fact that as consenting and loving adults you both deserve to have sexual enjoyment. He can help you fight any feelings of sexual inhibition.

Sometimes discomfort during sex comes from a much more obvious source. Sara had a question that might at first seem unusual, but actually affects many women.

Q Sara: Am I too tight?

Is there any way, besides having children, to help loosen your vagina? Whenever my boyfriend and I have sex, it always takes so long for him to actually penetrate me. It's like my first time, but every time – and not in a good way. Can this be fixed? I've never really discussed it with a friend and wouldn't know where to start getting help.

A Many women, mistakenly, will think that what you're experiencing isn't a 'problem'. They'll think they're *too* loose and wish their vaginal muscles were tighter. But to you this is a real problem.

Unfortunately you're experiencing something that quite a few women do, and like you they often feel unable, or too embarrassed, to speak to their partner about it. This means they suffer in silence every time they have sex. That's a terrible situation to be in and you must always be honest with a partner if sex is causing any pain.

You seem to have thought about this so I wonder if you've considered whether this is related to nerves and anxiety, or an actual physical tightness. Many women, when feeling anxious about sex, tighten up their muscles including their vaginal muscles. Once they learn how to relax and enjoy sex, and to trust their partner, then their muscles relax too. Do consider this and I hope you feel able to talk this through with your boyfriend.

If you feel it may be about anxiety or sexual inhibitions then you and he need to take your lovemaking right back to the foreplay stage.

If you believe it's a physical issue then it's best to consult your doctor. We are all constructed differently and in your case it might mean you're slightly smaller than the average woman, or have tighter muscles.

Steamy Sex Tip

You can introduce some deep breathing and muscle relaxation as you two simply caress each other. Build trust slowly between you. Don't rush into penetrative sex. You can always give him manual or oral stimulation to bring him to orgasm. And he can also bring you to orgasm in those ways.

Alice worried about the discomfort she experienced with her fiancé. But, as is often the case, she only felt discomfort sometimes.

Q Alice: Love hurts

Sometimes it hurts when my fiancé and I have sex. But other times there's no problem whatsoever and we have a fantastic time in bed. Is there something wrong with me?

A It depends what sort of pain you're experiencing. If it's during or after a vigorous sex session where you two have been at it like Olympic athletes, then it's not surprising you're experiencing a little pain. Many women experience a little bruising after such 'athletic' sex but this clears up fairly quickly.

Or if he's entering you before you're fully aroused and lubricated, it could be you're getting little tears and pulls in your vagina. If you think this is the case then always make sure you're ready for penetration after lots of fabulous foreplay.

Sometimes intermittent pain can be about a longstanding infection that flares up from time to time. So it's best to get it checked out with your healthcare provider or at a sexual health clinic.

Steamy Sex Tip

Once you've got your answer, always make sure you use a good-quality lubricant during sex play or if you use condoms, to use the lubricated variety. Turn using lubricant into a bit of foreplay where he sensually rubs and strokes it on you.

Miscellaneous myths, misunderstandings and mishaps

It's not just the myths about orgasms that can lead us to wondering what's going on during sex and with our bodies. We women often wonder about the things you'd think we'd know about. Here's a selection of commonly asked questions relating to myths, misunderstandings and mishaps when it comes to women, sex and their sexual responses, beginning with Julie's and Linda's different concerns.

 Julie: Am I normal?

I'm not in a relationship now, but I am enjoying sex with a man that I care about. He and I have an agreement about no strings (and safe) sex. What's bothering me is that sometimes I'm a little too wet. Does this mean there's something wrong with me? He doesn't seem to notice but I do.

A There's probably nothing wrong with you. Many women wish they had more natural lubrication, which is one reason why there are so many lubricants for sale. This tells me that your no-strings partner is doing the right things and your body is responding.

Relax and enjoy this. There would be cause for concern if your natural bodily lubrication became a discharge that was discoloured or smelt – in which case you should go to a sexual health clinic to have a screen for any infection.

If you're getting squelching sounds that some women find embarrassing then do some pelvic floor (Kegel) exercises to tighten your vaginal muscles. Not only do these exercises tighten your vaginal and pelvic floor muscles, but they also lead to more powerful orgasms.

For a basic set of exercises, squeeze the muscles that would stop you from urinating (although don't actually do this while urinating as you risk causing infections). Once you've identified those muscles, hold for two to three seconds. Do not over-squeeze. Repeat this 10 times. Then build these repetitions to twice daily, 20 times each session. You can do these when you're sitting at your desk, watching TV or any other activity like that.

Q Linda: Enhancing sensation

My husband complains that he can't feel me during sex, and I'm wondering if it's possible to have too much sex and stretch the vagina so it does not return to its normal size? Please help because this is really affecting our marriage. Are there any positions we can try to enhance the sensation for him? Is there anything I can do to make my vagina a bit tighter?

A It's very common for women to lose the elasticity in their vagina. Often this occurs either through age, after childbirth, gynaecological difficulties or surgery, or simply through muscle wastage because of lack of use. Even hormonal changes can make the vagina feel looser. You can certainly improve your vaginal and pelvic floor muscles by doing the Kegel exercises as outlined above. These will also improve bladder control.

You should see an improvement in a matter of a month or so. If not, ensure you do them properly. If you find these helpful you can move on to the more advanced exercises where you hold on to a vaginal 'egg', or love beads, clasping them inside yourself with your vaginal muscles. There are also vaginal weights you can squeeze and hold to further build up muscle strength.

Steamy Sex Tip

Any sex position that tightens your vaginal muscles will help. Many people find good old-fashioned doggy style – with their pelvis and hips pointed upwards – when they're on their hands and knees, naturally tightens these muscles.

Worries about pregnancy can also affect your sex life in different ways. It's not uncommon to find that a woman's inhibitions (or even a man's) revolve around a fear of pregnancy when they're not ready to have a child. In Helen's question, she is concerned about maintaining a round-the-clock sex life.

Q Helen: Contraception query

Can you get pregnant when you're menstruating? I'm definitely not ready to get pregnant now and my partner and I use condoms religiously. However both he and I would like a break from condoms during my time of the month. As we both had sexual health screens and neither of us have any STIs we'd like to have sex without condoms when we can.

A Technically you can get pregnant during your period, however this is fairly rare. If you absolutely don't want a child then you shouldn't risk having sex without condoms. I see you've found that rare creature – a man that isn't freaked out about having sex during your period. Many couples, who want to have sex all month long, choose to have sex in the shower to save any 'muss 'n fuss', but others simply put towels on top of their sheets so they feel free to get up to whatever they want.

Orgasms can help relieve monthly period pain. So if you're with the man who isn't interested in having sex during your period you can always enjoy some self-pleasure in a warm bath and your climax will give you some natural pain relief.

I get lots of women (and men) asking me about libido boosters for women. It seems only fair, considering men have Viagra, Uprima, Cialis, Levitre and others. Penny wondered about any new developments.

Q Penny: Libido enhancers

What's the deal with female Viagra – those libido enhancers I keep hearing about? I love my partner but I'm not always in the mood and this might be the perfect solution.

A To call something 'female Viagra' is misleading. There are lots of things available that claim to stimulate arousal and desire, but you need to be fairly careful what you believe and what you buy. Check with your doctor first about your testosterone levels. We think of testosterone as only being important to men and their sexual desire, but we produce it too. If your levels are low you can lose your libido.

Your healthcare provider might put you on some hormone replacement treatment if it seems advisable. Many women like the idea of what's called 'whisper cream' which is applied locally to enhance all-important blood flow to your genitals. On the commercial side there are all sorts of mail order and over-the-counter creams, e.g. Vigorelle, but most of these simply contain mild irritants like menthol and herbs. When applied to your genital area you get sensations of arousal (for some women at least) but for others it simply feels irritating. These sensations are fairly brief, lasting only a few minutes.

Other products come in tablet form, and include Avlamil, Avenavin and Therafem. When taking any such 'libido enhancer' ALWAYS discuss it with your healthcare provider first, as these commercial things might interact with prescription medications. Or they might have side-effects you should be aware of.

One natural libido booster is some simple romance and affection. When you're not in the mood, ask your partner to lavish some cuddles and hugs on you. Ask him to tell you why he loves you and what he finds attractive about you. He should really be heaping praise on you. Let him know that when you're feeling cherished you may just end up feeling in the mood. But then again you may not, depending on things like being too exhausted, having been up all night with the baby.

In Chapter 1, we looked at arousal and desire and from that I'm sure you could see just how big a topic it is. Part of arousal and desire is about initiating sex because when you feel aroused you're more likely to initiate it. Here, Jackie's question shows just why these things are important to consider in your sexual relationship.

Q Jackie: Initiating sex

When my hubby and I first started being intimate, he initiated sex much more often than I did. Now that we've been together a few years the tables have turned, and I'm the one who seems to want it more. I have tried talking to him about this, and he seems to understand, but nothing changes. I take it extremely personally when he rejects me, and I've let him know I feel this way. Do you have any suggestions for me to get the physical attention I need without him feeling used or pestered?

A Your story's a classic example of the myth that men are always more highly sexed than women. Most of us are used to the myth that somehow men always want more sex, but in my experience this is often far from the truth. What I find is that often men settle into their 'comfort zone' where they want less sex, often wanting the same type of sex (e.g. same position, same time of day), and they're very content with that. Then their partner is left feeling undesirable, sexually frustrated and wondering what happened to the man who used to want it more often.

Practically every couple goes through the 'honeymoon phase' where they can't get enough of each other. And as I already said that obviously needs to settle down – but there's settling down and there's disappearing. This is a classic dilemma where it's important to find a compromise with him. But first consider whether or not he could have some issue such as depression or stress that may be damaging his desire. Once you've considered such lifestyle/health issues, the next step is to rekindle a warm and loving feeling between you – as this might have caused some stress. Because you've managed to talk to him about it and he seems understanding, that's a good starting point.

At the same time it's also important to stop continually raising the issue of you feeling rejected. This can be a bit daunting to a man. He doesn't want you to feel that way, but he may feel helpless to stop you feeling that way. Instead try being a little bit romantic, as suggested, and trying the following without raising feelings of rejection should help.

Steamy Sex Tips

Why not rekindle old feelings of desire by revisiting some of your original haunts? It's easier to look at each other afresh when you've gone back to where you had your first date, etc. It can inspire some sexy flirting too – go for it and say some of the raunchy things you wouldn't have dared to say when you first met.

Try to tap into some of his secret desires. When you're both relaxed (and not stressed over this), whisper to him that you'd like to hear some of his secret fantasies.

Sometimes, even the person in the biggest 'comfort zone' will start feeling sexy when they're given permission to discuss their private fantasies. Encourage him to tease you with some suggestive snippets from his private thoughts.

Ask him if he's ever wondered about things like sex toys or other sex techniques such as a little bit of bondage-play (sexy techniques coming up in Chapter 5). Again, giving someone permission to get out of that comfort zone can work wonders.

One thing that's certain about women and their feelings about sex is that they're easily embarrassed about things which happen to so many people, and that they really shouldn't feel embarrassed about. Jemima probably thought she was the only person experiencing her 'issue'.

Q Jemima: Bodily noises

This is very embarrassing for me but I need to ask. When we have sex and my boyfriend enters me from behind and begins thrusting, I end up with air inside that comes out with a 'passing wind' sound out of my vagina. Not only is this noise embarrassing but it also makes having sex in this position painful. The problem is, it's his favourite position so I'm wondering how to position myself so that I don't get all filled up with air.

A Here are a few tips things to try, but first I want to reassure you this is a very common problem for women – they just don't talk about it. First off, sex shouldn't be painful so ask him to start thrusting more gently and more slowly. There's plenty of time for him to build up the speed and pressure of his thrusts. Anyway, most men and women would like sex to last a bit longer and this will slow it down as well as ensuring your comfort.

Also ensure you have plenty of foreplay so you're well lubricated. Use an over-the-counter lubricant if you lack natural lubrication. If it's still painful you should get your doctor/healthcare practitioner to check it out.

Next, by tightening your pelvic floor muscles, you may find it helps the trapped air issue. So do the pelvic floor exercises mentioned above. As these muscles tighten you're less likely to get air trapped inside your vagina.

If despite these things you still feel there is a build-up inside you of trapped air, you need to have the confidence to ask him to switch to another position where you're more comfortable.

Sex Doctor's Conclusions

We've covered a lot of dilemmas that particularly affect women in this chapter. Obviously these often affect their partners and it's the same in the next chapter, when I look at specific issues and dilemmas aimed at men – that can affect their partners too.

You might think I've left off real big issues that affect you as a woman. Perhaps your body image issues stop you from enjoying sex – that's to come in Chapter 5, when I'll look at men's and women's sexual confidence. Or perhaps you'd love some oral technique suggestions – again such things to come in the chapter on sexual technique. So be patient and I'm sure I'll cover your concern. Now to the men…

Chapter 3
Men's sex questions

At any given time, 40% of men over 35 find it hard to get an erection

The average length of time a man spends in full penetrative sex is two to three minutes

I'd like to stress again that with anything to do with sex between two people, there'll be many crossovers between what's considered the 'men's territory' when it comes to sexual dilemmas, issues or questions, and how it affects their partners. The particular details and things men worry about, though, are often quite different to what their partners worry about. And that's because we see things from different perspectives as men and women. I say, '*Vive la différence.*' Understanding your differences is crucial to improving your sexual relationship.

As in the last chapter about women, I'll tackle what comes up most in conversations with men about their sex lives, as well as what concerns women about their men.

A man and his penis

A good starting point is to get through the things that worry men most, and usually these are about his penis: the way it works, the way it looks, its size and attraction. Andrea asked about one of the things men fear most: being on the small side.

Q Andrea: Does size matter?

My boyfriend has a small penis. I'd hoped it wouldn't be a problem because the sex is good but I am afraid to try certain positions or certain things while we are having sex – I worry he might slip out and that would embarrass him. In some ways I might be the one who feels more uncomfortable about it and so I refrain from trying new things. But I know he is also uncomfortable with it. We never speak about it and I wish he knew that I love him regardless of the measure of his penis. How do I show him that but also get us trying new things?

A On the one hand I'm so glad that he doesn't have a complete small-penis complex that most men who are less well-endowed have. I say this because it sounds like he's fairly comfortable with what you two do, but that you want to try new things. The key here is confidence: yours about initiating new positions and techniques, and making sure his is high. When things are feeling good in bed between you, try relaxing and using a sexy tone of voice to suggest one of the things you've dreamt of trying. Only suggest one new thing at a time during a sex session, or else he might begin to think you're really unhappy with things.

For instance, let's say you've been fantasising having sex with him while standing up, with you leaning against the bedroom wall and he's behind you. You could say something like, 'I've got this amazing fantasy where we're really excited and sneak to the back of a restaurant, lean against a wall and have rampant sex.' How can a man resist trying if you suggest it like that, particularly when he's pretty confident?

It's simply timing and the way you say it that'll make this work best. If you've been kissing and caressing – and you know sex is on the cards – that's a good time. But if you're halfway through your usual position, that isn't a good time.

I think many men who feel they have smallish penises will identify more with Keith. Keith wasn't feeling as confident as Andrea's boyfriend.

Q Keith: Sexual confidence

I've got a complete complex about the size of my penis that's only about 10 centimetres long when erect. I know it's smaller than average because I checked this out. It means that when I'm in a relationship I won't start having sex until I really trust a woman – I'd die if I was laughed at. And it means I've had very few relationships because I lack confidence with women because of it. Apart from this I've got lots to offer and want to make sure my new girlfriend and I have a good sex life.

A I've always believed that size doesn't matter because some men who are well-endowed have absolutely no sexual technique or finesse in bed. Sometimes this is because they mistakenly believe that size 'is more'. Other times because they simply don't realise how to satisfy a woman, as many men don't. This means that a man who is less well-endowed can become the 'king of foreplay' and make up for any lack of size (real or imagined, because some men are a perfectly adequate size and think they aren't) by ensuring he gives his partner loads of pleasure.

Becoming king of foreplay begins with being able to ask a woman in a confident and caring voice where she'd like you to start with foreplay. There's no better starting place, but many men shy away from actually asking a woman what she wants. They feel they have to know instinctively how to satisfy women. Nothing could be further from the truth. Chapter 5 is full of sexual techniques – so don't forget that chapter if you want to become the king of foreplay.

It's important to see yourself as a complete man and not just a man with a certain-sized penis. Confidence is highly potent and if you're confident in yourself generally and confidently go about trying to satisfy your partner, then you'll be a success in bed and in relationships generally.

Maggie is married to a man with quite the opposite problem, he's too large for her to enjoy comfortable sex – or at least up until this point.

Q Maggie: He's too big.

My husband's penis is too long and this means sex is painful for me – not so much him. This makes it difficult because he constantly has to take care with how deep he goes inside me because when he goes in too far (forget all the way.) then it sends a painful spike through my cervix and stomach. Are there any positions we could try to make sex more comfortable and enjoyable?

A Don't worry as there are a number of positions you can try when a man is too large for your comfort. I think the best – tried and tested with many women having success with it – is you on top with him lying quite still. You can have your legs either outside of his (like a reverse missionary position) or you can have your legs between his. A key part of this technique is to wiggle up so your pubic bone is a bit higher than his pubic bone. Ask him to use gentle thrusts and circular motions and this means he will only penetrate you half way.

Another good option is to try the spoons position. Both of you lie on your sides with him behind you, facing you, and reaching around to hold you. This is a very comforting and loving position, you open your legs to allow penetration from behind – and you don't have to open them fully, so that prevents full penetration. Also you can reach around with your hands to push his hips slightly away avoiding full penetration during his thrusting.

But also try facing him, again lying on your sides. In this position you can also use your hands to hold his hips slightly away from you keeping some distance between your pelvises so he can't fully penetrate you.

With sex-perimentation you should find variations of these also work. Have faith as many, many couples overcome this when there's quite a difference between his penis length and her vaginal depth.

Steamy Sex Tip

If you try the spoon position, reach back between your legs so that you can caress his testicles while he thrusts.

Penises come in all shapes and sizes just as women's labia and vaginas do. Sometimes a man's shape makes sex a bit uncomfortable, as Josie told me.

Q **Josie: What positions should we try?**

My husband has a curve in his penis and although I know some curvature is normal his particular shape happens to make it difficult for us to have sex comfortably. What should we do? Can you recommend any positions or techniques?

A Again, I'm a doctor of psychology, not a medical doctor – but I recognise from what Josie said (and many other men and women over the years) that he may have Peyronie's disease. This is where fibrous tissue pulls the penis to one side or another. This can be corrected by a specialist. A man should consult his doctor to get a referral to a urologist for a consultation.

In the meantime it's best to experiment with different positions and use lots of lubrication to help. Any position where the woman is fairly 'opened up' will probably work best. So her being on top with her legs outside of his thighs is a good starting point. Or the classic missionary with him on top, but with her wrapping one leg around his waist to open herself up.

Steamy Sex Tip

He may want to try penetrating you from behind very gently so that he's in control of angling his penis in such a way that is least likely to cause discomfort to either of you.

A few penetrating facts

- The average non-erect penis is 8.5-10.5 cm long from base to tip (3-4 inches)

- The average erect penis is 15-18.5 cm long from base to tip (6-7 inches)

- Are you a 'grower' or 'shower'? A man on the smaller size of average *when flaccid* is likely to grow a full 100% when he becomes erect. When he's on the larger size of average *when flaccid* he's likely to grow by about 75% when he becomes erect.

The famous Masters and Johnson's sexual research team measured hundreds of penises, and the longest one in a flaccid state was 14cm (5.5 inches) long. The shortest was just over 5cm long (2 inches).

Men – take this on board: the average length of a non-aroused woman's vagina is 7.5 cm or about 3 inches. And when aroused, the average length is about 10 cm or 4 inches. So it doesn't take as much length to fill her vagina as you might think.

Maintaining his erection

Melanie faced a common concern that many women have when it comes to how long a man can keep his erection during penetration.

Q Melanie: How long should sex last?

In the beginning, my husband couldn't seem to last more than five minutes during sex. I thought that after we'd been married a while this would change, but it definitely hasn't. My friends tell me it means he's just sexually aroused by me and I should think of it as a compliment. But part of me wonders if it could be more of a problem. How can I help to make him last longer?

A On the one hand it's a fantastic thing to think a man is so aroused by his partner that he can't wait to have his pleasure. *Fantastic for him, that is.* Because where does this leave his partner? High, and dry, plus sexually frustrated. It's definitely time for him to have learned how to control his desires and I can't help but think this is selfishness or laziness on his part. And it's time he learned how to keep going for longer so that you have as much pleasure as he does.

There are many good things to get started with. The first thing is to recognise that this won't change overnight. Instead it will probably change in stages or small steps. Also right from the start, don't treat it as a criticism of him that he's being too quick. Instead when the timing is right, and you're cuddled up together, tell him that you'd like to take things slower.

Be playful and let him know that there are things you'd like him to do to you. The majority of men love to be given detailed instructions. The more detail that you put into this, the more likely he will please you. Take his hand and while holding it show him the sorts of pressures and caresses you want.

Steamy Sex Tips

You can even suck his finger to show him the sort of pressure you'd like on different parts of your body.

When he's focused on your pleasure he'll be less focused on his own. You can stroke his hair, his back, his chest, etc., but don't stimulate his penis or testicles. Keep him waiting. It would be a very positive step to ask him to bring you to orgasm before you even have penetrative sex. He can use his mouth, his hands and/or a vibrator. Once you've had your first orgasm you can then start penetrative sex.

Try to get him to last longer by changing positions or the things you are doing. Without even telling him this will actually slow him down. Imagine you're in the missionary position and then you teasingly tell him how much you'd like to try doggy style. By simply moving around to behind you, he stops getting immediate stimulation.

Finally, if he learned to strengthen his pelvic floor muscles (the ones he'd use to stop himself urinating, just as we women need to strengthen ours) then he can pulsate those when he's getting near to his own climax. Please read on to see about my special 'tea towel' test for these.

Sometimes a man simply needs time to develop awareness of his bodily responses, how to control them and ensure he satisfies his partner. Lily discovered this in her relationship.

Q Lily: How can I delay his orgasm?

My husband and I have recently got married – most people thought we were too young to do so as we're both 22. However, we're both very mature in our relationship and it's only in the bedroom that I think his age matters, as quite often he reaches orgasm before I do. Is this something I can expect to change as he matures?

A At this time of life a man begins to develop the maturity to recognise that he should take time over sex. He becomes more concerned with his partner's pleasure and not just with his own. Most men in their 20s know full well when they've climaxed too quickly and fret over how to stop this. They still may not have the communication skills, though, to handle talking about such concerns so they sometimes end up with performance anxiety. Unfortunately this doesn't help premature ejaculation – and it can make it more likely. As in Melanie's story above there's lots that can be done – and regardless of whether a man is in his 20s, 30s or 40s you can apply those steps.

Always let a man know in a warm, loving and sensual way that you'd like to try for a second time around. Coming across in a demanding way might be a bit intimidating for him.

Finally, an important point to make – particularly as we're dealing with a young man here – is that premature ejaculation is often due to 'habits' left over from youth. Many men have felt pressured to rush sex in their first sexual experiences. And these can set the scene for future sexual experiences. Remember, having once worried that their parents might burst in on them when they were having sex with their girlfriend, their body gets used to speedy ejaculation.

Steamy Sex Tip

Why not have full sex once, having told him you're going to expect a 'sexy second time around'. Not only can most men in their 20s manage a second time around within 20-or-so minutes of ejaculation, but they're more than happy to accommodate you this way. What's the great thing about 'seconds'? He'll be much slower reaching his own climax, giving you time to reach climax this time around.

There are many things affecting a man's ability to control himself. Some quite surprising, as with lifestyle stress. Sophie's question illustrates this.

Q Sophie: How can I make him last longer?

I'm 26 and my fiancé is 36, and we need a bit of help. I hardly ever get to orgasm because he gets too stimulated too quickly. He's always been under a lot of stress, so I guess I can understand his bouts with erectile dysfunction (ED). He's been getting erections fairly regularly since we've been trying to get pregnant, but he just can't last long at all. I've worn little sexy outfits, but that adds more stimulation for him. Help please.

A As with any one – man or woman – who is under stress and it's affecting their sexual enjoyment, he needs to identify how he can reduce that stress. In the meantime show enthusiasm by helping him masturbate. Yes, you might be thinking this is rather kinky but there is a real point to it. You can help him learn about his 'point of no return' – the point just before ejaculation where nothing would stop him ejaculating.

Once he's used to identifying those signals, encourage him to stop stimulating his penis (or you stop if you're doing it for him) until the moment passes. Then he/you can resume stimulation until the moment arises again, and when he'll then pause again. Doing this a few times a week will help him build control over ejaculation. Put this new knowledge of his into practice with penetrative sex. He can let you know when he's nearing that point of no return and withdraw, while continuing to stimulate you with his hands or a vibrator. Once he's regained control, he can start thrusting again.

Many men who come too quickly need to develop strength in their PC muscles. He can exercise it by squeezing it 10 times, holding for two seconds each time, and repeat twice a day. Pulsating them slows down his orgasm. He can repeat pulsing them as often as he wants during penetration. Let him know it'll make his orgasm more powerful when he gives in to the desire – a great incentive to draw it out.

Steamy Sex Tip

Have fun encouraging him to try 'Dr Pam's Tea Towel Test'. Get a tea towel and slip it over his erection. Ask him to try to 'bounce' it up and down a few times. He'll get better and better as you applaud his achievements. Now that's a little bit of kinky fun that'll have you both giggling.

Such a workout increases his pelvic floor, or pubococcygeal (PC) muscle strength that he can use to slow down ejaculation. If he squeezes his PC muscle (as with us, the ones he uses to stop urinating) at this point, this will stop him climaxing as long as he's not got to his 'point of no return'.

It can be extremely anxiety-provoking when a man can't maintain an erection, let alone climaxing too quickly. Karen got to the point about her concerns over her husband.

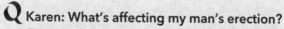

Q Karen: What's affecting my man's erection?

Recently my husband – who isn't very old at 36 – hasn't been able to maintain his erection. What could be the cause?

A One in ten men experience some type of ED at some point in their life, and this rises in the over-35s. Usually it's transitory but it can rock his confidence. It might happen after heavy drinking, drug taking, as a side-effect of medicine, or due to medical complaints like diabetes. It can be emotional, though, and in about 40–50% of cases, emotional issues and stress cause ED. For example, he's too stressed at work or is worried about your relationship. Sometimes it is in response to a lifestyle choice like drinking heavily the night before and only occurs after that.

If he can get and maintain an erection during masturbation, or if he wakes with a morning tumescence (erection), then it's likely to be emotional/stress related. Suggest he tries masturbating to see if he can get erect and maintain it. Many men need their partner's 'permission' so they don't feel guilty. If he can't get erect on his own he should go to his doctor and discuss whether any medication he's taking has this side-effect or whether he needs to be checked for, e.g., diabetes or circulatory problems.

I hope you're talking about it and not sweeping it under the carpet. Some loving words can go a long way. He can check for nocturnal erections with the 'postage stamp' test. He can paste a ring of stamps around his penis at bedtime and if it's broken in the morning you both know he's had an erection. However, if he moves a lot during sleep that may also break the ring anyway.

If he gets early morning erections or when masturbating, then together you and he can talk things through about where the stress may be in his life. Reassure him that you don't see this as a problem but as part of life, and together you two can get to the bottom of it.

Sometimes partners are so concerned about a man's premature ejaculation that they're desperate to do anything to help, as Emily wanted to.

Q Emily: Getting the spark back

My husband struggles with premature ejaculation that has completely knocked his confidence. What can I do about this? I'd do anything to restore his confidence as I love him so much.

A Along with the advice above, you can do some key things to help. For your part, you need to build his confidence generally. Outside of the bedroom make sure he feels like a man that's valued and needed. Bolster his confidence by praising the great things he does. Inside the bedroom let him know how much he pleases you when he focuses on your pleasure.

Then share with him the information I've given about pelvic floor muscle strength and control, and tell him you'd love it if he'd use masturbation to get to know his own body signals. By using these techniques and focusing on your pleasure (so he's not thinking about how excited he feels) he should gain more control.

Steamy Sex Tips

In a sexy voice, tell him you'll take control through some fantasy role-play. Pretend you're his boss and he's your personal assistant. You've asked him to stay after work to help you with a special 'task'. Then continue with fantasy chat describing a scenario where he has to do exactly what you tell him so he's completely focused on your pleasure.

To help slow him down gently tickle his 'million-dollar spot' located on the central area on his perineum (between the base of his testicles and anal opening). As you gently circle and stroke this area whisper to him to fight his sexual urge by 'pulling' in the muscles of that area – as if to pull away from your fingertips. This is a fantastic way to build his PC muscles that'll help him control his ejaculation. It'll also feel amazing to him.

Slip a well-lubricated condom on him to decrease his sensitivity. Have fun doing it, be playful and tickle his testicles while you slowly slip it over his penis. Once on it'll decrease his sensitivity particularly if you use one of the heavier-duty condoms.

Keep the focus on your stimulation so he's focused less on his. Kneel over him as if you and he were in '69' position. Suggest that he gives you a great big helping of oral sex since he'll have fantastic access to you. But instead of giving him oral sex back – because you want to slow him down – simply tease his million-dollar spot with gentle vibrations from a vibrator so he doesn't get overexcited.

I'm frequently asked what one crucial piece of advice I'd give for premature ejaculation if I could give only one. Samantha asked me just that.

Q Samantha: How do I delay his orgasm?
What is your best and most unique piece of advice for a man who wants to last longer in bed? What should he do before and during sex to delay orgasm?

A I believe the key advice is to give the man back his physical control. And he can definitely do this by doing the exercises described earlier to increase his PC muscle strength for staying power. Everyone – men and women – should have strong PC muscles.

Steamy Sex Tip

Definitely turn PC muscle strength into sex play. Both men and women can start pulsating these muscles during penetration to slow him down, give both stronger orgasms, and give a thrilling sensation to each other.

Robert was concerned about his performance with his new girlfriend. As soon as the man gets concerned about his sexual performance, it's very likely to affect his erection, as Robert found.

Q Robert: Desire has turned to anxiety

I've been with a new girlfriend for two months now and have completely fallen in love with her. She's amazing – not sure what she sees in me – and I see her as potential wife-material. I can't figure it out but when we started sleeping with each other six weeks ago I started to lose my erection. I'm desperate to sort this out.

A This sounds like a clear-cut case of performance anxiety particularly as Robert stressed how amazing this woman was. Often a man's beliefs about his desirability, including thinking someone is 'too good for him', can lead to such anxiety.

Although women can get anxious (sometimes very anxious) about how good they are in bed, performance anxiety can have a profound effect on a man and his confidence – both overall and sexual confidence. Because, quite frankly, we can see right before our very eyes the evidence of his anxiety: he doesn't have an erection.

A good starting point for helping him over his performance anxiety is to encourage a much more relaxed approach to sex. When a man responds in a worried, anxious way to losing his erection it's crucial his partner doesn't heighten this sense of failure. Using calm and confident tones she can express affection and caring. Sometimes with this soothing reassurance a man will regain his erection and other times it's far better to let sex 'go' at that time and enjoy some simple affection.

A man needs to give his partner some guidance about whether he wants to continue trying to get an erection or whether he'd like to relax and just have some hugs. If both people are prepared to speak out tactfully – the man with guidance about how it's affecting him and the woman with reassurance – things can be sorted out.

It's important to realise that he may not feel *at all* sexy. But a partner can still subtly let him know that she finds him desirable by giving him compliments, and letting him know that he's important to her whether or not they finish having sex.

Sometimes this may be the perfect situation where taking a sex sabbatical can help. You take the pressure off a man and his sexual performance, by suggesting that you two have affection only for a few weeks or so. If it's psychological, and not a medically related loss of erection, then this can do wonders for him to feel he doesn't have to try again straight away.

Steamy Sex Tip

Sometimes adding a bit of spice through fun 'sex chat' – where you're allowed to tell each other your secret desires – lifts the mood if he's experienced ED. As you describe what you fantasise about, suggest slowly 'doing' whatever it is. Give each other 'permission' to touch each other as you're describing fantasies and he may find his desire returns as he gets into this.

Making condoms sexy

There are many passion killers as far as a man is concerned. Eric described a classic situation where using condoms might kill off the passion a man is feeling at that moment.

Q Eric: Condom passion killer

Every time I put on a condom, my hard-on begins to wilt. What can I do? I feel terrible as I don't want my girlfriend to think it's about her and whether or not I find her attractive.

A You're in good company, many men experience this and it's purely psychological. And you're right to be concerned that she might think it's about her – and potentially thinking you're not sexually attracted to her. We always want to blame ourselves for such things.

Your erection won't wilt if you develop what I call 'Condom Confidence'. First off, when on your own try a variety of condoms to find which brand fits best – snug enough not to leak but not so tight it ruins your pleasure. Practise with them during masturbation. This will raise your confidence when with a lover.

Without practice you might fumble and feel inexperienced. There's nothing wrong with inexperience (we all start out inexperienced.) but it can kill the moment.

Steamy Sex Tip

Turn using a condom into sex play asking her to slip it on you when aroused. If she fumbles, you can take over and slip it on with skill.

Make condoms more sensual by putting a drop of condom-friendly lubricant in the tip before slipping it on. Not only will you look like a skilled lover but it'll feel so much better. Enjoy practising.

More 'Condom Confidence' tips

This gives me the perfect opportunity to suggest that all readers – men and women – get condom confidence.

- Don't forget your nails and teeth can pierce condoms, so handle them with care.

- Practise how you approach using a condom with a new lover. Don't believe any excuses for not using them. Men in particular try things like, 'don't you think I look clean?' The cleanest 'looking' person in the world can still have a sexually transmitted infection.

- Be ready with a confident reply along the lines of, 'I care about both of us and so insist that you wear a condom.' No 'glove', no 'love.'

- There shouldn't be an argument in this day and age when STIs are rife. If there is an argument about it, they aren't the right person to sleep with.

- Keep your condoms with you at all times - it's common sense.

- Finally read the instructions on any new brand of condoms you buy. For example, some are more durable and better for practices like anal sex.

Erectile difficulties aren't always about not being able to get one or to maintain one. Teresa found that her husband's erection went on and on.

Q Teresa: Turning my man on

Sometimes my husband does not orgasm. It makes me feel abnormal – like I'm not turning him on enough. I've tried to ask him if there is anything I can do, but he insists it is him and not me. I have offered to try anything, but I'm constantly rejected. Is there anything I can do to make him orgasm faster or sometimes orgasm at all?

A This sounds like a case of delayed ejaculation. In reality more men than you'd think either don't reach orgasm all the time or take a very long time to do so. With delayed ejaculation a man has a fully functioning erection, but there are various reasons why sometimes they have had difficulty ejaculating.

It can be a sign they've had too much alcohol or used illegal recreational drugs. They might simply be overly tired or stressed or have certain circulatory problems. In a case like Teresa's he might insist it's 'his problem', but it makes a man's partner concerned – so it's her problem too. When both of you are relaxed, and have some time, let him know that you'll do anything you can to help and you don't want him worried about this on his own. Tell him you're not worried about it, as long as he's not worried about it. You can also say that sometimes sex is just about sensual touching and foreplay, and not always about orgasm. Couples can forget this most basic fact. Then leave it for a time. You can only say so much and then it's important to relax about it yourself. In the meantime try to ensure you both get quality time *when rested* before you have sex.

If you have any suspicion that there might be an underlying medical cause, then a man with delayed ejaculation should check this with their doctor.

Steamy Sex Tips

Some men confide that they need a very particular sort of stimulation to ejaculate. They feel embarrassed to ask their partner for the exact stimulation they desire. So if you have any suspicion that he needs or wants some particular sex technique (lots on technique in Chapter 5), then ask away. Tell him you're dying to know what might really get him super hot.

One technique guaranteed to speed up his climax is to slip your finger into a condom (as you'll have noticed they have many other uses besides safer sex and preventing pregnancy) and super-lubricate the end of it. Then slowly and sensually tease his perineum with stroking motions from your fingertip. You can even stick the tip of your condom-covered finger slightly up his anus and tease this area with tiny strokes. Believe me he'll be ready to explode with excitement.

Get him super excited before you even start sex by wearing a dress or skirt without any knickers on. Cuddle up to him – maybe as you watch TV – and put his hand between your legs. Get him to tease and tickle you as you tell him about your fantasy to be a really naughty 'tart' who never wears knickers and is always up for sex. He may want to take you right there and then on the sitting room floor.

Other classic concerns men have

Ageing has a lot to answer for. Often worries and concerns are thrown up in a sexual relationship simply because of a matter of age. Cindy was concerned about her long-term partner's fear of ageing.

Q Cindy: Maintaining desire

My long-term partner and I are in our late 40s. Our sex life has always been very satisfying, but recently he has started to fear losing his sexual power and attractiveness. Is there anything that can be done in this situation?

A Losing sexual prowess is something many men and women worry about. It's the rare person that isn't fazed by ageing. Begin by ensuring that you both look after your physical health: eat well, sleep well, exercise and de-stress your life. Downsizing any area of your life that makes you feel pressured, like working long hours, is a good idea if you can.

Then you can also reassure him that you still find him desirable. When you're both fit and well – and showing your love and affection for each other – you'll enjoy keeping that spark alive. And he'll be less likely to worry about his sexual prowess.

As a couple grows older together they may both be getting aches and pains, possibly weight gain, which can all contribute to a sense that you're 'past it'. Be honest about the changes you're both going through and have a sense of humour to take any fear out of it.

Finally, it's a good idea if a man gets his testosterone levels checked, as these lower from about the age of 40, affecting desire. These can be topped up and that can make all the difference.

Steamy Sex Tip

Take him on a walk down memory lane to rekindle passion. Make a reservation at the first restaurant you had dinner together at. Or even book into the same hotel you spent your first night together. Surprise him by wearing an outfit in a style that is sexier than you normally wear. And remind him of the first time you two had sex – of course in loads of detail.

We all know the saying 'familiarity breeds contempt', and it can also breed boredom in the bedroom. Carl was concerned about this, as so many others find in a long-term relationship.

Q Carl: Relighting the fire

I love my long-term girlfriend very much but if I was honest things have got stale in the bedroom. I worry about suggesting new things as she's quite sensitive and she might get the wrong end of the stick and feel I'm criticising her. What's the best way around this?

A Oh dear, here's that resounding theme again – when a partner makes a suggestion about something in the bedroom, we always think it's a criticism of us. We point that finger of blame at ourselves and think, 'I'm not exciting like I once was, I'm not attractive any more, etc.' So if we want to change things we often feel like Carl did – that it may not be worth trying if our partner reacts badly.

I'll go into more detail on bedroom-communication techniques in the next chapter, but the best starting point is always highlighting something that you love or at least like about your sex life. If you make your partner feel good and desirable because you're highlighting what's going right, it'll be easier to go on and suggest something new.

Steamy Sex Tips

One night when you're both relaxed, play a game of 'truth' where you each have to write a list including three things: one new sexual position you'd like to try, one new place you'd like to have sex in and one new sex toy/ item you'd like to buy. Then exchange lists and take turns over the coming weeks fulfilling these. If you're feeling less confident, simply put one or two things on your list.

Sometimes the easiest way to try something new is to simply 'lead' your partner into it without saying anything. If you're stuck in one or two tried and tested sex positions – and you're getting bored with those – guide your partner with your hands and body into another position. You can pre-research sex positions – and I highlight some of the hottest in Chapter 5 on improving your sex technique.

Even small changes such as if you usually make love in the evening then swap to the morning can make a difference to keeping a little fire burning for each other.

Making things hotter

We often accuse men of simply wanting fast, lustful sex, but William wanted to satisfy his wife in a more sensual way. And I find many men share his concerns and they don't want to be seen as overly assertive in the bedroom.

Q William: How can I be more sensual as a lover?

My wife and I haven't been married for a very long and I love her to pieces. Her ex-husband was a bit of a brute and always got his way in the bedroom. I definitely show her lots of respect but also wonder how I can be a bit more sensual in the bedroom as I'm not that experienced.

A There are lots of ways to develop the sensuality between you. Begin by taking the 'goal' out of sex as being all about orgasm (something most of us buy into – the 20 seconds of orgasm versus the 20 minutes of foreplay that we should be enjoying) and instead enjoy the path to getting there.

Suggest and enjoy some SEPs – what I call 'simple erotic pleasures'. Try shampooing each other's hair with sensual strokes. Lovingly caress the shampoo through each other's hair in turns. Even if it doesn't lead to full sex it'll lead to soft hair. Try the same with having a bath and tell her you want her to laze in the bath while you sensually wash her hair – and body – and then she can do the same for you. Towel each other off and simply caress each other in bed or on the sofa.

Steamy Sex Tips

Definitely try little things like hand-feeding her with things like luscious, creamy desserts. It's very sensual to be hand-fed some rich chocolate mousse. And if you've got the opportunity then take this sexy food-play into the bedroom. Smooth some of that luscious dessert onto her nipples and gently lick it off. This may be a cliché but it definitely hits the spot.

Never forget the importance of whispering words like, 'I love you', and 'I think you're beautiful', to a woman. When you seduce her mind you seduce her body too.

As with many women who need specific stimulation to reach climax, some men can only climax in a specific way. Jenny asked about her partner's need for oral sex.

Q **Jenny: Alternatives to oral?**
My partner's only able to orgasm during oral sex. He tries and wants to climax while inside me, but he hasn't yet. He withdraws and I give him oral stimulation. He doesn't have trouble sustaining an erection, so I was just wondering if there is something we can try for him to achieve an orgasm without oral stimulation.

A The first thing I always ask in these circumstances is does he have any concern about you getting pregnant? Some men who are worried about pregnancy end up subconsciously stopping themselves from ejaculating during penetration. I say 'subconsciously' because sometimes they're really not aware that they're doing this in reaction to their fears of pregnancy. Not climaxing during penetration reassures them that pregnancy won't take place. However, even if he doesn't ejaculate, a woman can get pregnant through *any* penetration as a man will produce seminal fluid containing some sperm when excited.

If you two haven't discussed this then it's time that you did so in a loving and caring way, rather than a threatening way. If potential pregnancy isn't troubling him then you'll need to explore other things, like does he have an issue over the 'mess' after he ejaculates? Some men have such concerns.

Another fascinating area to think about is that some men have a deeper emotional fear of intimacy – and for them ejaculating during penetration symbolises this. They feel they've given away too much of themselves in an intimate way.

There's much for a couple to think about. When you're both feeling relaxed, try raising these various ideas with him in a tactful and gentle way. Finally, if after such conversations he still cannot let go and ejaculate it might be worth seeing a sex therapist. However, if he satisfies you with penetration, and then withdraws before he ejaculates, who says there's anything wrong with that?

Just as when a man loses his erection, it's important not to pressure a man who has delayed ejaculation or who can only ejaculate in a very specific way. Pressure simply exacerbates what is happening. Patience and gentle exploration is the way forward.

Steamy Sex Tip

Why not vary this routine you've got into? Discuss the following sex-periment you're going to try in advance. Suggest that you two enjoy penetrative sex until you climax and then he withdraws as he usually does. Give him some oral pleasure but as he nears his 'point of no return' ask him to go back inside you.

It is quite normal for men, women and couples to experiment when it comes to trying different aphrodisiacs to heighten their sexual experience. Andrew wondered about trying Viagra.

Q Andrew: Will Viagra give me more powerful sex?
What happens if a man with a normal, functioning sex drive takes Viagra? I don't have any problem getting an erection but I wondered if using it might heighten the experience I have with my wife.

A Some men with a normal sex drive report that Viagra gives them a more intense experience. However, why risk the side-effects if you've got a normal sex drive? Viagra is a drug meant to help those with erectile problems and was not intended simply for recreational use. So be warned.

Steamy Sex Tips

If you want to heighten your orgasmic experience in a fantastic and definitely safe way, why not try some pelvic muscle squeezes during sex as already mentioned. If you 'work' that penis – really pump those muscles – you'll have a much more powerful orgasm. Lots of sexy techniques to follow in Chapter 5.

Something guaranteed to give you a more powerful sex-perience is to put a blindfold on, and try and guess what she's touching you with. Is it her tongue, lips, or her fingertips dipped in lubricant?

Ask her to do the 'Oriental slide' technique – super hot, and it'll get you wanting steamy sex. You should lie flat on your back, she sits astride you with her labia well lubricated, and then she slides them back and forth along the shaft of your penis. Top her up with more in lubricant using your fingertips.

≈

> Ask your partner when you are caressing her, if there's something she'd like to try to heighten both of your pleasure. She might feel the same way particularly if she is aroused and feels more confident to make some suggestions.

Men are often more keen to explore every part of a woman when they have got the confidence to do so. Amber wondered if her boyfriend was a little bit overenthusiastic.

Q Amber: Touchy subject

My boyfriend likes to touch me everywhere and with all parts of his body. During foreplay he plays and rubs against my body. And sometimes he wants to put his penis between my breasts, between the cleft in my bottom, will rub it over in my thighs, etc. It's like he's one great big touching machine. I quite like it but wonder if this is normal sexual behaviour?

A Men find it a huge turn on to get inside every nook, cranny and crevice your body has to offer. They want to enjoy every inch of you. Different parts of you will yield different sensations as he rubs against you. And men are always looking for a new sensation – just the way we might. Help lead the way and guide him into the crease under your breasts, between your inner thighs, turn onto your stomach and allow him to nudge between your buttocks, etc. He'll love it.

Steamy Sex Tip

Use lashings of lubricant all over your body so you can slip and slide together as you experiment with touching each other all over your bodies.

Always keep in mind that your bodies are one big blank canvas to enjoy. People usually focus on one or two main erogenous zones during foreplay, forgetting the rest of the pleasure centres we all have including the highly sensitive areas – behind the knees, inside the wrists, along the ankles and behind the ears.

Men also want you to enjoy every inch of them. Roger wanted his fiancée to run her hands *all* over his body.

Q Roger: Stroke me all over

I'd love it if my fiancée would let her hands roam all over my body. She zeros in on stroking my chest, moving her hands down to my stomach and then between my legs. It feels fantastic but I feel she's missing a lot of my erogenous zones…so I'm missing out. I don't really want to ask her to touch me in different places because then I'll feel like I'm being demanding in bed.

A

In the next chapter on communication techniques and building sexual confidence I'll cover many tips and tricks to encourage more sex-ploration. But for now it's key to understand that she simply doesn't realise that men have more erogenous zones than just their chest and genitals. There's so much written about women and their many erogenous zones that we girls are guilty of forgetting you men have many too. When she's stroking your chest tell her it feels great and ask her to continue that stroking on your lower back, bottom, neck, earlobes – wherever you like to be touched.

 ### Steamy Sex Tips

How about standing 'erect' when it comes to exploring each other's bodies? Be bold and have naked, standing-up sex. You probably have horizontal sex most of the time. And you might never have had upright-sex, made even more erotic with nothing on. There's a whole different feeling when you explore each other's bodies while standing – it gives you a totally new sex-perience. You can run your hands all over each other – even more so than when you're horizontal.

If getting naked and showing the effects of gravity on your body seems a bit too daring, why not slip on blindfolds? You can use a silk tie or scarf. You'll still enjoy standing up sex without feeling shy.

Another technique you can use to encourage her to explore more of your body is when you're exploring hers, comment about how it would feel good if she'd touch you in the same way. It'll dawn on her that as you discover her erogenous zones she can also discover yours.

Men and masturbation

One topic that troubles many women is men and masturbation. Many women often just don't get that most men masturbate simply *because* they masturbate, or for sexual tension release. But women often assume it's a statement about their desirability rather than the men's desire. Sometimes there's justification for concerns about a partner masturbating too much, as Karen felt.

Q Karen: Self-pleasuring, why does he do it?

My husband and I have only been married for six months now, and I already feel like our sex life is suffering. We sometimes go several days without having sex, but he masturbates daily. Often he does so when I'm at home with him. This makes me feel so hurt – like I'm not enough for him in bed, or that he'd rather masturbate than have sex with me. When I raised it with him he just doesn't seem to see the problem. How can I make my husband choose sex with me over masturbation?

A I can see why Karen would get worked up about this but still it's probably that his masturbation is simply a habit of a lifetime and so he doesn't see it as a problem. Instead it's just something he does – *very* regularly. He also doesn't have the sensitivity to see how you take this personally – that he continues to masturbate and yet you often go without sex together for days.

First it's important to realise that many men use masturbation as much for tension release as sexual pleasure. You need to think about whether or not this is simply a tension release 'exercise' for him, or if he does it for sexual pleasure. If it's a tension release for him, you need to have a tactful conversation about him doing other tension-burning activities like going to the gym or doing sport.

If it's sexual for him, then again you still need to have honest and non-heated conversations about how this makes you feel. Once you get to the bottom of why he masturbates frequently you can then start to move forward. It's important for him to gain more understanding about your feelings. You can try the empathy-approach of asking him how he'd feel if you masturbated daily and then ignored him in bed. Encourage him to put himself in your shoes. He needs his eyes opened to this.

I always say that masturbation is not a problem unless it's upsetting someone in a relationship – as in Karen's case. Or it can be a problem if it's jeopardising a person because they're doing it at inappropriate times or places. So bear in mind these two things when it comes to men and their masturbatory habits.

Steamy Sex Tip

Ask him to show you how he strokes himself. Not only is this a great 'learning experience' about the sort of touch he likes, but it can be super hot too.

Women sometimes seem surprised by some of the sexy suggestions their partner might make, or desires he has. Rosie thought her partner needed far too much 'extra' stimulation in their sex life.

Q Rosie: Dirty weekends away

My partner seems hung up on getting away for dirty weekends – it's as if he needs extra stimulation or to feel that we're doing something naughty. I've spoken to my girlfriends and some of them think their husbands could turn any 'away day' into a dirty weekend. I just feel so much pressure that everything has to be perfect when we go away on a special weekend – but he doesn't seem to feel that way.

A Many men don't stress about things having to be 'perfect' the way women often do. They relax and think, 'let the hotel staff clean up our mess – let's just have fun.'

When women let go of those issues they usually relax and enjoy going for a hot weekend the way that men can. And once they do that couples definitely feel and behave differently when they're in hotels, as all of our senses are bombarded with fresh things – a new-look room, crisp sheets, maybe fresh flowers, and all sorts of complimentary goodies in the bathroom. Add to that the sense of luxury when ordering up some room service consisting of food-to-get-rude-with and you can pretend *anything*. It's the perfect 'excuse' (not that we should need one.) to try new sexual techniques and positions.

To ensure your dirty weekend lives up to its promise, start *slowly* and indulge yourselves with that precious commodity – time – that we so rarely have. Take a leisurely bath or shower and as well as soaping each other up with the luxury bath products, take time to sensually wash each other's hair. Use the huge, warm towels to caress each other dry and then stretch out to linger over your room service.

Steamy Sex Tips

You're not washing the sheets so have fun with food. Sprinkle drops of bubbly over your lover's body and lick it off gently. Spread some creamy yoghurt and honey over them and lap off the drips. Call each other by made-up names to give the sense that you're both up to no good. And then get up to no good – on the floor, in the bath, on the dressing table and against the wardrobe.

In this period of economic recovery many couples can't afford to go away for weekends in hotels, but there's no reason why you shouldn't plan a dirty weekend at home. Agree to switch off your phones and fib to people, telling them you're away. That way you're less likely to get bothered anyway. Then enjoy indulging each other in ways you don't normally have time for.

There are men want to try out new stimulation like a dirty weekend, and there are others who are happy with their tried and tested sex routine that can be frustrating for their partners. Sandra felt that her long-term boyfriend had blinkered vision when it came to seducing her.

 ### Sandra: Dirty but not sexy

My long-term boyfriend's room is so dirty it turns me off sex. He seems not to notice it and would be quite happy to jump on me when his flat looks like a pigsty. I find this a complete turn off. What's going on here? Is he just being a typical man?

A Many men have a knack for switching off to 'extra' stimulus (including certain visual stimulation) when they have sex on their mind. All they can think about is their goal, and that goal is having a good time. Forget about the mess around their bed, what counts is the sexy woman on their bed.

A messy room may seem a minor transgression in the grand scheme of sexual relationships, but men should realise that women can be distracted by such things, no matter how great your seduction technique. Do an extensive spring clean and get it sorted out, once and for all. It may not sound very sexy, but if you clear out the clutter in your bedroom, it'll feel more inviting and you two will be inclined to spend more time in there.

Even women can be guilty of paying too little attention to their bedrooms compared to how much attention they give to sitting rooms, or even kitchens. That's a real pity as the bedroom is where we are most intimate with each other. Get soft-tone lightbulbs for the bedside lamp for a more flattering glow, and create a 'comfort zone' with scented candles too – lavender or vanilla are two smells that have been shown to increase penile blood flow.

Remember that although you don't make the connection between the way your bedroom or flat looks and how you feel sexually, your partner may well be affected in this way. This is a good example for that important 'sex rule' – we all have different needs, desires and things that get us turned on. The fun is in finding out what works for a partner.

Steamy Sex Tip

Having a seductive-looking bedroom – and even a seductive corner in your sitting room – where you've got access to candles, music, soft cushions, etc. increases your chances of sex play. Always have 'beforeplay' – a term I coined a number of years ago – at the heart of your thinking and how that gets you both in the mood. Beforeplay involves all those things that create a feel-good comfort zone in your relationship.

Playing with porn

Probably the trickiest area where women have anxiety about men's sexual desire is when it comes to pornography. There's so much potential for misunderstanding between men and women when it comes to why a man likes to watch porn, or the sort of porn he likes to watch, when he likes to watch it, etc. It goes without saying that many women enjoy watching porn too, but there's still far more chance of issues arising over a man and his interest in it than vice versa, as in Jamie's question.

Q **Jamie: How can I get her to enjoy porn with me?**

I like watching porn and would like my long-term partner to enjoy it with me. I see nothing wrong with porn, especially as I only look at it once every couple of weeks. It's not like I've got some sort of porn problem. She doesn't seem to have much interest but I wonder if there's a way I can get her interested.

A Some women clearly aren't interested in porn – there are many reasons for this: they may believe it's offensive, or perhaps feel threatened by the overly enhanced women in porn, or simply don't find it a turn on. It's crucial to get to the bottom of her feelings and why she's not interested. It might be that she feels inhibited about expressing a desire to see porn. She might worry you'll think she's a bit too kinky.

Always begin these conversations in a neutral environment – in other words, no porn flick on in the background. Let her know that you are completely open-minded about what her honest feelings are. If she's a little bit curious about watching porn it's definitely a good idea for her to choose a female-friendly film to start with. There are various companies that produce couple-friendly porn, like the films by Anna Spam.

Steamy Sex Tip

If she agrees to watch porn with you don't forget where your attention should lie – on her. There's a definite etiquette to watching porn with a partner – you don't get so glued to the film action that you forget to hold and caress your partner. Always check if your partner wants you to pleasure her while she's watching the film – many women find it exciting that although there's a porn film playing their partner is paying attention to their needs.

Keep it hot

Let's continue with a bit of porn etiquette: never compare a partner to someone you've seen in a film, always make your partner feel valued when you watch porn rather than feeling ignored, when suggesting that you both try out something you've seen in the film, make it about doing something that gives your partner pleasure, rather than trying to recreate what you saw a porn star doing. Also never pressure your partner to watch porn and if they enjoy occasional porn then keep it just that – an occasional spicy treat rather than something you watch every time you have sex. Never underestimate how much your partner might compare herself to women in porn films, so be tactful and don't marvel at how sexy you find them.

Sex Doctor's Conclusions

Having spent time looking at some of the most frequent questions I get asked about men and their sexual desires and worries, it becomes obvious that men are every bit as complicated as women. Nowadays, though, we're more likely to read about women's issues, like finding it hard to climax or a lack of sexual desire. The balance seems to be tipped towards women, and obviously, these are important issues to get out in the open so women can enjoy sex. However, it means that the many areas where men may experience sexual difficulties are sometimes pushed aside.

I hope this chapter has demonstrated that men have a variety of feelings towards sex and with just a little time and effort (and without anxiety) these can be understood. It is just as important that the man enjoys a sexual experience as much as the woman does. Of course, many men have very straightforward sexual feelings and can be fairly easily pleased but even when they're not experiencing something like ED (erectile dysfunction) there may be times where they need special attention to meet their needs.

It's now time to look at how you can communicate your needs in a positive way to a sexual partner. And we'll also look at how to build your sexual confidence.

Chapter 4

Your sexual confidence and communication

Only 23% of couples say they communicate well in the bedroom

13% of people say that the words 'I love you' put them in the mood for sex

It'd be foolish to think that your sex life isn't profoundly affected by the way you communicate with partners and also by your confidence – particularly your sexual confidence. As with all the following chapters, practically all of the following suggestions and strategies *apply equally to men and women*, no matter who has asked the question – whether male or female.

Let's first look at common queries when it comes to your sexual confidence. Believe me, as it increases so does your ability to communicate with your partner and get what you want out of your sex life.

Your sexual confidence begins with how you feel about yourself and feeling that others value you. Mike asked a particularly poignant question – and funnily enough one that women normally ask me.

Q Mike: Loving words

I know my wife loves me but she never tells me or make me feel that I'm needed or wanted. This really affects my confidence particularly in bed as I started to doubt that she finds our sex life any good.

A Two words spring to mind: appreciation and praise – when a partner feels appreciated and is praised for the good, loving, sexy things they do, their confidence grows. It's like watering a flower but with love and attention. If a person doesn't get that praise and appreciation, they start to wilt inside. They lose confidence as you have, but there is a lot you can do to turn this situation around.

Sometimes partners need a direct nudge to let you know that they're valued. Tell her how much you love her and what you love most about her, and also how desirable you find her. Hopefully she'll respond with praise and appreciation for you. But if she doesn't, you can ask for it. We're so frightened of asking for praise and appreciation because it makes us feel vulnerable. You'll never increase your confidence if you don't learn to ask for these things because many people (including your partner) simply don't offer such appreciation without being nudged.

Also, sexual confidence is definitely bound up with general confidence. So everyone should day-by-day remind yourself of your good points. Talk yourself up with a positive voice that gets rid of that negative, doubting and critical voice we all tend to have in our head.

As well as asking your partner for praise and other lovely things that make you feel good, you can remind yourself of your great qualities. Think-in-ink, and write down your three best qualities on a Post-it note. Put this where you'll see it every day.

 Steamy Sex Tip

Tell your partner why you think they're sexy, desirable and attractive. Everyone, men and women, love to be complimented. Give them some hot, juicy detail like telling him how fantastic his penis feels inside you. Or telling her how fabulous it feels to be inside her.

An issue that practically every woman and man will identify with – in some shape or form – is body image issues and how they damage your confidence making you feel *un*sexy. Tania's question is fairly typical of the ones I get asked.

Q Tania: Confidence booster

How can I boost my body confidence? I'm not in a relationship right now but I do have issues about touching myself (I don't masturbate) and letting a partner know what feels good.

A Let me reassure you that many people feel this way about their bodies. It's an excellent starting point that you recognise you need to change this. Start off by giving yourself 'permission' to get to know your own body. Tell yourself it's okay and completely natural. If these feelings have sprung from the way you were raised (many parents have a lot to answer for in this regard) remind yourself that they came from another generation that was inhibited in this way. You are not part of that generation and you do not have to feel inhibited about anything you do with yourself in private.

The person that pleasures themselves through masturbation will know what to share with their partner. This is crucial to enjoying your sex life. Affirm to yourself every day all your great sexy features, e.g., your wicked smile or naughty glint in your eye, and your willingness to learn about sex.

Each day take a few moments to lie back, close your eyes and visualise yourself as a Sex Goddess, or Sex God for men. Hold this wonderful picture in your mind. Put in as much detail as you want and bring this image to mind when you know you're going to see your partner.

Practice makes perfect when it comes to body confidence. So if you've got a new sexy outfit, practise – on your own – taking it off slowly – you don't want to get stuck over buttons and zips when you're with your lover.

Remember that the person you end up in bed with probably has – or has had – similar issues with their body or sexual confidence. We all worry about these things – it's just whether we let such worries take over our feelings, or if we talk ourselves into feeling more positive.

Steamy Sex Tip

When it comes to how you feel about the way your body looks, definitely accentuate the parts of your body you like by selecting sexy clothes that show off those parts. Flaunt what you've got.

Body confidence tips for everyone

Here are top tips to help banish those body hang ups in the bedroom:

- Always emphasise your sexiest attribute – whether it's your breasts, bottom, legs, shoulders, back, etc. We all have at least one attribute we know is attractive. And why focus on the ones you're not so happy with when you can flaunt the one you like.

- Ensure you turn your best attribute into an 'erogenous zone' and ask your partner to caress and kiss it.

- Next, stop any negative thoughts about your body. Remember your partner's with you, aren't they? And your partner can feel they're with either a gibbering wreck who worries about their body, or with the confident person who knows what you do is more important than that bottom you wish was smaller.

- Train your mind so that you feel sexier, e.g. because you 'weave' sex into your normal life by wearing nice underwear to work, etc.

〰 Occasionally run your fingers down your erogenous zones (not necessarily through a full masturbation session) and feel how great your skin is to touch – and how much your partner will love it. Taking a moment each day to feel sensual develops your natural sensuality.

〰 Finally, as a woman don't get hung up on your bedroom-body. Men don't notice our lumps and bumps, they're far more forgiving of these than we are.

At times, our sexual partner may be more concerned about our lack of confidence and what they can do about it – as Justin below.

Q **Justin: How can I turn my partner on?**
My wife is not very sexually active now and wasn't even before we met. She doesn't feel comfortable about her body and appearance and has low confidence generally. This is all getting in the way of getting going sexually. What can I do?

A The great thing is you've identified that she has low self-confidence, so as a starting point you need to help her boost her confidence levels. Take sex off the agenda for the moment, and look at activities and hobbies that make her feel good about herself. Give her loads of praise and compliments. Suggest she becomes her own 'confidence coach' and learns to talk herself up if she's got a negative voice in her head saying that she's not a very good or attractive person.

For fun you can encourage her to go to a department store and get one of their free fashion makeovers. Also a new haircut and make-up can make a woman feel fantastic, especially when you tell her she looks amazing.

Get more romantic – make little romantic gestures each day that help boost her confidence. Such gestures only need to be small like compliments, love notes, candlelight at dinner, buying her a romantic CD, etc., but they can really make a person feel valued and good about themselves.

Steamy Sex Tips

Tell her that nothing would turn you on more for her to ask you to do exactly what she wants you to in bed. Really make her feel confident that you want to please her. And that you need her guidance. Dim the lights and don't look directly at her when you're asking her to describe what would turn her on.

Play a little game of 'Dare'. Tell her that you'll flaunt your body and walk across the room in your underpants, if she'll do it. Turn it into a bit of fun, but maybe begin with her simply sitting on the bed in a sexy new bra and underwear set. For people with body issues that would be a big challenge.

One thing that definitely boosts bedroom confidence is to create your own hot 'signature sex technique'. I suggested this to Elizabeth.

Q Elizabeth: Self-esteem boost

I've been working on building my confidence in the bedroom with the help of my boyfriend. He's incredibly loving towards me, and it's not his fault that when we met I was feeling pretty bad about myself. I'd love any special suggestions.

A I think it's a super hot idea to devise your own signature sex technique. This can really boost your confidence and you can claim it as your bedroom 'signature dish', so to speak. Think about what you like doing most when it comes to sex. Maybe you're a good kisser or your partner tells you that you give a very sensual massage, etc.

Think through what twist you can add to this thing that you already do well. For instance if you're a good French kisser, you might want to try gently flicking the end of your tongue inside the edge of your partner's lips. This is a highly sensitive area that rarely gets stimulated.

Steamy Sex Tips

Take something you do well to a new and more daring level. For instance, if he loves the way you grip, squeeze and stroke his hips/buttocks during penetrative sex, why not suggest fingering his bottom. Slip a condom on your finger, and with lots of lubricant stimulate this sensitive area.

Also have fun with your surefire sex technique – tease your partner and say that they'll get your special technique if 'they're good, and behave themselves'.

Seven steps to losing your inhibitions

Here are some tips to help throw you into sex full-throttle and lose your inhibitions.

💨 Forget your exercise class, instead take lap dancing or strip lessons. This is a sexy way to lose any body inhibitions, with the added benefit you can put a show on for him one night. Not only will he love the sight of this, but you two can also work up a fantasy scenario around it. He can do a full monty too.

💨 Take a picnic out to your favourite beauty spot and go skinny-dipping with your partner. Fresh, whirling water helps loosen any inhibitions.

- Do something childish like going to a theme park or fun fair. Shrieking with delight and having a giggle helps you break free of adult anxieties and responsibilities.

- See a scary movie together. All the excitement and unexpected twists and turns will make you ready to jump into his lap and abandon any worries.

- Get a sexy mascot who you emulate/pretend to be. Think about your favourite celebrity and how their confidence means they can flaunt their body down the red carpet. Keep a mental image of them in mind and affirm to yourself that you can flaunt yourself in the same way.

- It's very important to have a fun and carefree attitude when having sex. Not only does it show that you're prepared to let go with your partner - and so trust them - but it also shows you've got good sexual confidence. Your sexual confidence is bound to rub off on them making them a better lover too.

- Establish a 'love zone' in your bedroom where you can be confident that everything is to hand for creating the right mood. Sensual candles and matches, a mood music CD, some sexy things to throw on, etc. This will boost your confidence when you two find yourselves in the mood and do not want to rush around looking for those matches.

Ruby was worried about her husband and his method for gaining more confidence in the bedroom.

Q Ruby: How can we get hot without getting drunk?

My husband only seems to enjoy sex after he's had a few drinks. I worry this will become a problem for him. What's this all about, doesn't he find me attractive?

A This is definitely about his lack of sexual confidence, and not about your desirability. Many people rely on alcohol to loosen inhibitions so that they can enjoy sex. What they need to do is to learn to enjoy sex when sober.

Try some sexy moves on him when you two haven't had any drinks. Always be aware of opportunities to do this or to discourage any excess drinking. Apply any of the confidence-boosting tips in this chapter with him.

Never forget that you shouldn't drink too much before having sex – a little alcohol relaxes your inhibitions – too much takes desire away. Or it might even lead to 'brewer's droop' in men.

 Steamy Sex Tip

Why not suggest a leisurely breakfast in bed – you're both relaxed after a good night's sleep. Get into spoons position, with him behind you and both on your sides. Then wiggle your bottom into his genitals, sigh and murmur how good you feel. Hopefully he'll be up for some sober fun.

Sometimes you might push a partner too far, hoping to build their sexual self-confidence but finding that they simply say no to your suggestions, which is what happened to Henry.

Q **Henry: Role-play too far?**

I find my fiancée incredibly attractive but she's not all that confident. I'm dying to try a bit of fantasy role-play with her but when I suggested it, it was obvious she thought that was a step too far.

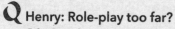

A You're right to think fantasy role-play can boost sexual confidence – and be sexy fun of course. But you can't push someone straight in to it. The reason it can help with confidence is that by having a bit of fantasy chat or role-play allows you to let go of emotional and sexual inhibitions – as you play that role you're not being yourself – and that's quite freeing.

Also some sex therapists believe that women take on one role in relation to their sex life (like the role of someone who is always pursued until they say yes to sex) and stick to it. A little role-play can release them from this and allow them to explore and enjoy other roles.

Armed with this knowledge you can use the advice given in Chapter 6 on fantasy role-play to seduce her into this.

Sexual confidence begins by knowing what you like and don't like. And many people who lack confidence will say no to something you suggest. Beware that it might be a lack of confidence behind this rather than them really not wanting to try it.

Steamy Sex Tip

You can always say something about yourself in a fantasy role to stimulate their interest. In this case why not say you imagine yourself as the handsome police detective who comes to interview her after her house was broken into. Then give a little detail about how you seduce her – that might help her change her mind.

What we think other people are doing in their bedrooms can make us feel bad about our own sex lives, as Nancy asked.

Q Nancy: Is my sex life hot enough?

My best friend seems to have a wild sex life compared to mine. I love chatting to her about these things, but sometimes it leaves me feeling a bit useless in bed. Should I pick up some tips from her?

First off, we definitely shouldn't believe everything that our friends say about their sex lives. Most people embellish and exaggerate what they get up to. Take what friends say with a pinch of salt. Second, don't buy into the myth that just because your friend enjoys something, e.g., she swings from chandeliers, that it means you're going to enjoy the same thing – it doesn't. Give yourself the right to be your own person with your own desires.

Never allow your own confidence to be affected by what you hear about sex. People have such different needs, desires and sex drives that there's absolutely no point comparing yourself to someone else. Make this a hard and fast rule for your sexual confidence.

Steamy Sex Tip

If a friend does mention that they had, say, amazing oral sex - by all means ask them what made it so amazing and you may just pick up a really hot technique.

Communication in the bedroom and beyond

Now let's take a look at improving your communication skills in the bedroom. Samuel asked a classic question about sexual communication.

Samuel: Why can't she tell when I want sex?

I've lived with my girlfriend for six years and she still doesn't seem to 'get' when I'm in the mood. I would've thought she could sense when sex is on the cards but she doesn't seem to pick up my signals. Any suggestions?

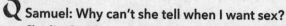

Remember, neither you nor your girlfriend is a mind reader. In fact men are notoriously worse at picking up these signals, so I'm surprised you're expecting her to do so. For all you know she's sending out signals that she's not in the mood – that you're not picking up.

It's not that you have to go up to a partner and say, 'let's get to it.' But if clear flirting signals aren't getting your message across then use this more subtle way to bring sex up. Remind your partner about the last time the two of you had sex together. You can say how 'great' it was and that you've been thinking about it. Then try a suggestive smile and knowing look – and if your partner still doesn't grab the bait then ask if they want to 'recreate what you did the last time'.

Just as you can't expect your partner to necessarily guess when you're in the mood, you can't expect them to guess how to satisfy you. Yes, you might have had lots of sex but always guide them into what would 'do it for you' at that particular time, just as you'd like to know this for them.

Sometimes when you need to discuss something with your partner, it's better to underestimate the issue as I recommended to Vanessa.

Q Vanessa: Is he bored with our sex life?

I've been married for 10 years and I recently have worried my husband is bored with our sex life. I simply don't know how to raise my worries.

A It's important with certain worries about sex – like whether your partner's bored with you – not to exaggerate your worries, and if anything to play them down, the key being not to blow them into a bigger problem. Always raise such concerns when out of the bedroom, when you're both relaxed, and in a confident tone. If you use a confident tone of voice then your partner will sense it's not such a big deal and you have the confidence to get over it.

Sometimes by not raising these things you exaggerate worries like that your partner might be bored with you. The more you think about them, the bigger they get. And you may be making a mountain out of a molehill.

 Steamy Sex Tip

In a situation like this it can be best to be a bit flirty. You turn on the charm and flirt-factor and say something like, 'I've wondered recently if you'd like to try some new things in the bedroom.' This technically solves the problem of boredom, without actually mentioning the word boredom.

Part of great sexual communication is sometimes about 'doing' something rather than 'saying' something, as I recommended to Tammy.

Q **Tammy: Weighty issue**

Before we got married I noticed that my husband started to put on some weight. He's not tremendously overweight, but I'm sure he's depressed about it and we haven't had much sex since our honeymoon. When we do, it's always when he wants and never when I want it. He says he can't stand his body and it's too much work for him to get aroused.

A Unfortunately this is all too common a cycle when it comes to weight and worry about your attractiveness. He's ended up in a vicious circle with putting on extra weight taking away from his feeling of desirability. The less desirable he feels, the more likely he is to comfort eat, then he puts on more weight and ends up feeling depressed, and so on.

The good news is this cycle can be broken with love, understanding and introducing a new regime into your household. Begin by getting him out for 'fun' exercise together. Start gently, going for walks (before vigorous exercise someone who's very overweight should see their doctor). Then take up an active hobby together like dancing, swimming, tennis, sailing, bowling – whatever you two enjoy.

It's time to tackle your cupboards. Stop buying fatty or sugary items. Make sure your fridge and cupboards are stocked with healthy foods.

As he talks to you about his body image that's another positive. Ask him to turn to you for a quick pep-talk when feeling down. Just a quick phone call or email – once he learns to talk rather than 'feed' his emotions he'll be on a better path.

Now for your sex life: keep the talking going, letting him know that as he starts feeling better having sex may be more appealing. Emphasise your supportiveness of him and ask in return that he shows you more affection and love. Make it clear that you'd like more compromise between you. Also make it clear that sometimes you'd be happy with some foreplay, rather than full penetrative sex. Other times you'll want the whole shebang. A happy sexual relationship between you two will be one where you understand each other's needs and are prepared to give-and-take where necessary.

When it comes to this particular issue of weight gain and sex – it definitely can make someone feel depressed. Again, this should be checked out with a doctor. It may be once someone's more active and eating better they'll start to naturally feel better. But if depression has 'got hold' they might need treatment through their doctor.

An important element of bedroom communication is showing your partner you're having fun, as Simon asked.

Q Simon: Sexy fun

What are some ways to show my new girlfriend I'm having fun in bed with her?

A There are a number of great ways to show a partner you're having fun. Show her some clear visual cues through your facial expressions – these will tell her how you're feeling – relax, smile, and allow your pleasure to shine through.

Next use your vocal cues – the sighs, moans and groans – those 'sex sounds' unique to everyone – that'll express how you're feeling and turn her on at the same time.

Also by showing her you want a repeat performance – a second time around – you clearly signal how much fun you've had.

Show your partner you're having fun by telling them you're having a good time and that you want to return the favour.

Steamy Sex Tip

And if you feel like getting vocal, be playful with it - give your penis a nickname like 'the stallion' and tell her that the stallion is feeling 'very happy'.

There are so many things we potentially want to bring up with our partner about sex – some serious and some small. I've devised clear steps to take, and shared these with Alexandra.

Q Alexandra: Let's talk about sex

What's the best way to bring up a sex issue with my partner when I know he's quite sensitive, and I don't want him to think I'm criticising him?

A The best possible starting point is always to think of a positive to say first. Compliment them on something they do really well. Tell them you want more of that. Once you've got that conversation going, you can compare this to the thing that you don't like in a subtle way by saying, 'I've found that doing A, B, C is more satisfying than X, Y, Z.' This makes a simple comparison that is said with confidence and won't be taken badly.

Golden rules of communication for getting what you want

Now is a good point to give you my golden rules:

- Always begin on a positive note – like saying how much you enjoy the way your partner, e.g., kisses your breasts. You can then say what you'd like to try that's new. This way they feel happy about what they're already doing, and more likely to want to try other things.

- Show by your behaviour what you might want to do differently. So let your fingers do the 'talking' and start touching your partner in a way that suggests trying something new. You can avoid upsetting your partner by, say, not suddenly whipping out a great big vibrator. But instead ask if they'd like to shop for one or include using one in some fantasy chat and see their reaction.

- Show your partner where else you'd like them to touch or caress you. Even during full sex you could slip a vibrator between you for new sensations during thrusting.

- Always use the guise of playing a little sex game to introduce a new tip, trick or technique. Why not show your partner some dice, suggesting that you take turns rolling them. Each number represents a new sex technique to try.

֍ It's a good idea to take conversations about any tricky things out of the bedroom. That way the bedroom isn't associated with these sometimes difficult conversations. Set a subtle atmosphere when trying to discuss an issue or get them to try a new technique. Taking it out of the bedroom doesn't mean it has to be in the brightly lit kitchen. Dim the lights or light candles, have some soothing music on, and over a glass of wine begin the conversation.

֍ If you have something positive to say and it's simply about wanting to try a new technique, suggest it when you're relaxing or having a warm cuddle. Or you can ask them what 'secret' sexy things they might want to try. Opening the door for them to tell you what they think about in this relaxed context gives you the chance to share your secret ideas.

֍ When you want a partner to stop something they do, for instance, you don't like the way he spanks your bottom during sex, say something like, 'It seems fun when you spank me but it kind of distracts me from reaching orgasm.' If you can put things this way around, finding that positive angle, you can make your point.

֍ When on your own, rehearse what you'd like to say. By rehearsing you gain confidence. Also always use vocal techniques that sound confident like lowering your vocal tone, and speaking a bit slower. Be confident that you can gauge your own partner's reaction to being asked for something new – many love it when asked to try something specific – it helps them stop worrying about how to please you.

֍ Always use special events like birthdays, anniversaries, etc. to suggest something special you want to try. Put it in the context that you'd like to give them a special pleasure to celebrate.

֍ When you bring up trying something new, never make it sound like the old thing was completely boring.

🔥 You may be valid in thinking your partner always wants to do the same thing. But remember that accusing a partner of never wanting to try anything new - even if it's true - will stop any progress in its tracks.

🔥 Show a partner this book (or any other sex guide) while casually chatting - ask if they'd like to browse through it with you. Spice things up and suggest opening a random page to try a suggestion from it.

🔥 Take an occasional 'refresher' weekend together and use that as an excuse to try a new tip, trick or technique. Having different surroundings puts people in the mood for doing something different.

🔥 Boost your chances of getting to try new things by turning the spotlight on your partner and their satisfaction. They'll find it a turn on when you ask them what they'd like to try.

Sometimes something as simple as wanting to have sex in a different place can make someone anxious. Sophie wanted to suggest just that.

Q **Sophie: How can I move sex from the bedroom?**
My boyfriend and I always have sex in the same place – our bedroom. I'm getting pretty bored with this, but wonder why he hasn't suggested anything. Could it be he only feels comfortable having sex in bed?

A Location, location, location – it's important. We're guilty of being incredibly boring in our choices of where to have sex and forget that variety is the spice of life. Finding somewhere new to have sex means not only being visually stimulated by the new surroundings (and we know what visual creatures we are.), but more importantly, couples get a buzz from the sense of adventure.

You're also more likely to shed normal inhibitions. A new place equals a new frame of mind where you two can indulge each other in new techniques. You might even pretend you're strangers on the pick-up for some truly raunchy sex that you wouldn't try at home.

 Steamy Sex Tip

Use your ingenuity – if you're planning a day out, pack everything you'd need to have some 'alfresco' sex: a blanket or a towel, Wet Ones, even sun block. Once there, it becomes a *fait accompli* when you suggest a fast sex session.

It's difficult talking about tricky sexual issues, and Ellen was worried about this.

Q Ellen: He doesn't turn me on any more

I'm not sexually satisfied with my husband. I've tried everything – lingerie, books, flat-out telling and showing him what to do – and I just don't know what his problem is. Things are just so boring in the bedroom. I'm beginning not to feel sexually attracted to him. He says that he tries to be better, but it just isn't for me.

A Such issues can cause anger, and you sound quite angry. This makes me wonder if something else's going on in the relationship and you're using not having satisfying sex as the focus of the problem – when really something else is bothering you. This is more common than you'd think.

Perhaps there's a power struggle going on in your relationship. Or you feel you do the lion's share of the chores, etc. Maybe he annoys you in other ways. In that case it's easy to look at a partner and think there's no point trying anything else. Or maybe things are okay in the relationship and really it's a difference in your sexual expectations.

Only you can decide whether these sorts of issues are where your lack of satisfaction began. When it gets to the point of no return (i.e., you don't satisfy me no matter what I try) a negative cycle develops. He feels defensive because he thinks you're on the offensive.

First, draw a line under how you've been relating recently. Suggest a 'sex-free sabbatical' (mentioned in Chapter 1) to take the heat off the sexual side of things. Then build more loving feeling between you.

Do that with these: make a point of complimenting him each day and asking him for a compliment in return. Next, do a little favour for him each day – even if it's simply leaving a loving note on his pillow or sending him a loving text. Go out for a weekly date and do something fun like seeing a movie or eating in a new restaurant. Over four or five weeks see how this works in terms of getting back a loving feeling.

Once you both feel more loving, that'll give you confidence to explore more of what's happening with sex.

Steamy Sex Tips

Think back to something he's told you about sex that turns him on. Do that for him. By being sexually generous with him he may try even harder to meet your needs.

If you haven't, masturbate to find out what really feels good and works for you. Then take this new self-knowledge into lovemaking and describe in lots of detail *exactly* how you want to be pleasured. If these things don't work it's wise to consider marital counselling when things in the bedroom are destroying the rest of your relationship.

Sex Doctor's Conclusions

Overall it's probably best to think of building both confidence and communication as a step-by-step process. These things can seem extremely daunting within an intimate relationship and it's very common to ask questions like, 'how do I tell/ask my partner this-or-that without offending them?' It seems like an enormous task if communication has been tricky or neglected, to turn it around and improve it. The same goes for your sexual confidence and also helping to build your partner's confidence. It might seem impossible until you break it down, a bit at a time, and then it will definitely improve.

Having given you lots of suggestions and strategies to improve your sexual confidence and communication, now let's turn to your bedroom technique.

Chapter 5
Your sex technique

41% of people report that massage/caressing techniques get them highly aroused

20% of couples now use oral sex techniques for complete satisfaction

In previous chapters I've touched on a few sex techniques relating to some of the common dilemmas I've answered. Now we can get straight into the common worries people have when it comes to their sex technique and keeping a partner satisfied. Let's begin at the beginning, with touching techniques. And let me remind you that the majority of these techniques apply equally to men and women and their erogenous zones.

Let your fingers do the talking

Women have twice as many nerve endings in their skin than men, making it super sensitive. Merely brush against a woman's skin and it can jump to life. But men also enjoy a full range of pleasure from being touched. Josh was concerned about his new girlfriend's sensitivity.

Q Josh: How should I touch her?

I know women are very sensitive when it comes to being touched. I'm with someone new and would love some suggestions for how to make her feel good during foreplay.

A I'm glad you are thinking about her sensitivity. With that in mind you need to think about your hand care – something most men never think of. It doesn't reflect on your masculinity to make sure your hands aren't rough. Before you see her, always trim your nails, as jagged nail edges will catch her tender skin. Also make sure you buff any calluses regularly to keep them under control.

In private you can moisturise your hands with hand cream (there are plenty of male grooming products on the market) to keep them moderately soft. Before you start touching her in foreplay warm them under warm/hot water. Always keep asking her if your touch feels good. As she gets more turned on, check that she doesn't want a gentler or firmer touch.

As you get to know her body more and discover her erogenous zones, here's a fabulous touching technique that feels incredibly sensual. Imagine that you use your fingertips like little raindrops, in a 'pitter-patter' pattern of tiny raindrops landing on her skin. This technique will get her turned on as you move this pitter-patter sensation down her stomach and right across her pubic mound.

To get your fingers placed correctly, think of this area as being about a hand's width below her belly button and about 1.5 centimetres above her clitoris. Your fingertips can pitter patter lightly back and forth across her pubic mound. Underneath this area the clitoral region extends down under her labia, and across her pubic bone. Most people think of the clitoris as just the small 'bud' at the base of the pubic mound, above her vaginal opening. However, the discovery of the 'clitoral arms' shows that underneath the skin this sensitivity extends outwards. So the raindrop technique stimulates this whole area. It sends out tiny vibrations that can drive some women nuts. She might want full penetration much sooner than you think with this technique.

Steamy Sex Tips

After using the raindrop technique, and when you can feel her mounting excitement, simply start gently moving your fingertips back and forth across her pubic mound. The change in sensation feels wonderful. But there are so many places to try the raindrop technique and then to swap to this gentle back and forth movement - so enjoy trying it on all of her erogenous zones.

Now you've got in mind looking after your touching tools (your hands.), think about intensifying her pleasure when she's touched. You can maximise her sensual experience by bringing her skin to life. And a super sensual tip to do this is to offer to help exfoliate her skin.

Why not do this in a sexy shower, with a face cloth covered in some body scrub. Gently use circular motions with the face cloth to exfoliate her skin. It feels fantastic, and most women are surprised when a man suggests this pleasurable technique. Or have her lie on a warm towel placed on the bed as you gently use a body brush across her skin in long, gentle sweeping motions. This will get her nerve endings 'prepped' for the most amazing foreplay.

Men of course love to be touched in different ways, but often women aren't sure how to get started. Kathy wanted to try sensual massage on her fiancé.

Q Kathy: Tips for a sensual massage

My fiancé brought home some massage oil but I really don't know how to get started massaging a man's body. No previous boyfriend has asked me to do this.

A Although men are slightly less sensitive than women, they love all sorts of touching techniques. Use a basic swirling technique to get started. You can practise different sensations on your inner wrist – try tracing tiny figures of eight in circular swirling patterns. You can gauge how sensual that feels. When it comes to using this on your partner you can vary the intensity, the speed and the size of the little swirling patterns you make with your fingertips.

While you vary your touch, you can get an idea of how your partner is feeling through the noises he makes. This swirling pattern is great on smaller erogenous zones. If you're in the middle of foreplay you can do this swirling while you're kissing. And do it anywhere from inside their wrist, the back of their neck, around a woman's breasts or across a man's chest, etc. Move that swirling up their arm to the inside of their elbow. They'll probably never have had such a delicate touching sensation in this little-touched erogenous zone.

Steamy Sex Tips

It goes without saying to use this swirling technique across his groin, between his thighs, etc. If you've stopped massaging and are getting into foreplay, then use little swirls as you kiss. A whole section on oral sex techniques is coming up, but you can definitely combine kissing your partner's lower abdomen and thighs while you also swirl your fingers around these areas.

And for the man – if you're kissing around a woman's pubic mound and labia, why not gently push her legs open and do these tiny figure eight and circular swirling patterns very high up her inner thigh where it meets the beginning of her labia – pure heaven for her.

Try a larger variation of this massage technique called the 'Erotic 8 Massage'. This will give a lovely pleasurable sensation, but in a different way. Have your partner lie on their back. Warm your hands by rubbing massage oil between them, and start with your hands meeting at their breastbone. Sweep your hands outwards and apart along the sides of her breasts/his chest and bring them inwards, meeting at the belly button. Then swirl back outwards around the sides of their hips, coming in to meet at the top of their pubic bone.

Next, repeat this movement but in reverse, moving back up their hips having your hands swirl back in to meet at their belly button first, and then out again and around the side of her breasts/his chest and ending with their meeting at the top of their breastbone. As you can imagine this makes a big figure of eight on their body. Continue to do these big swirling figure of eight motions up and down their body.

For added pleasure, have them turn onto their stomach and recreate this sweeping figure of eight massage technique from their upper back down to their buttocks. Come in at their waist and then sweep back out and downwards. Pause when you get down to their buttocks - where they meet and slide your fingertips down to where their upper thighs come together. This is a very sensitive erogenous zone - pause there, letting your fingertips caress this area before repeating the figure of eight massage.

Sometimes we just know our sex life needs spicing up and want to kickstart it with one new technique. This is what Tim asked.

Q Tim: Hot sex surprise

I've been married for seven years, and it's not that I've got the seven-year itch or something but I know things could be a bit hotter in the bedroom. I'd love to surprise my wife with some new sex trick.

A I'm always happy to hear people wanting to surprise their long-term partners with a new trick or technique. Because putting in a little effort will reap rewards. One surefire sex technique guaranteed to set her heart (or his heart) racing is 'feathering'. This technique is definitely erotic and pleasurable – with hardly any effort on your part. You need massage oil, a feather, and your partner's willingness to lie back and enjoy.

This technique goes hand-in-hand with any other foreplay and kissing and caressing – and will definitely help take things a bit further.

Your partner lies back after you've removed her top. Warm some massage oil between your hands and gently stroke this up and down and around their chest, breasts and stomach. Now you take a clean feather (available from adult or artist supply shops) and begin by gently swirling the tip of it through the oil.

Then you can move it back and forth, up and down, landing on particularly sensitive areas like teasing your partner's nipples (guaranteed to send her and even a male partner to heaven) with the tip. Add extra oil as and when you need to.

Steamy Sex Tips

Work the feather and massage oil down their body and ask them to part their legs. Apply more massage oil to their inner thighs and run the feather up and down, and around and around this entire erogenous zone. This will heighten their pleasure and builds excitement because it's a very teasing technique.

For an alternative pleasure you can use this technique with practically anything that comes to hand. Obviously take care and be sensible with any sex play, for instance you don't want to use anything like an empty champagne bottle to tease your lover with. But other things can add to your touching techniques like the innocent kitchen basting brush - rougher than a feather but still pleasurable, particularly for someone who likes a firmer touch.

Things like a kitchen basting brush can lead to some spontaneous sex play. For instance if you're having a candlelit dinner, you can start a bit of sex chat with your partner. Toy with the basting brush, flirt and tease. Then unbutton their blouse/shirt and with a little bit of olive oil (handily there for your salad), brush some on and slide the basting brush across their breasts/chest.

Being a bit spontaneous like this can really spice things up. You can laugh about it with your long-term partner the next time you are at the kitchen table, saying, 'remember the time you took me on the kitchen table after spreading olive oil all over my breasts with the basting brush?' And that's how sexy memories are made.

Too many people feel they're a bit useless when it comes to trying new ways to satisfy their partner. Most don't realise only a little bit of creative thinking can make all the difference, and Michael was no different.

Q Michael: How can I spice up my love life?

I'd love to try out some new moves on my wife. I love her so much but sometimes think I'm not very good when it comes to doing new things in bed.

A I always say a good starting place for trying something new is not to make it difficult. And one of the easiest touching techniques – 'The Alternator' – can give lots of good sensations to your partner. All you do is alternate which hand you use to stroke and caress your partner – and build up their excitement. 'The Alternator' is great to try on their larger erogenous zones, for instance, a woman's breasts, and for either sex their bottom, belly and inner thighs.

Definitely get lots of lubricant on your hands and start stroking the area to be massaged. For a female partner have her lie on her back and gently start massaging her breasts, then begin this technique. Massage her breasts with one hand and then slip that hand out of the way, as you slip your other hand onto her breasts. Alternate the direction each hand moves, with one moving downwards and the other moving upwards as they take turns stroking any erogenous zone.

As you alternate your hands, why not plant a few kisses on the area you're massaging – or near to that area. Then move your alternating hands to another area such as their stomach or inner thighs. When you do the alternator on this area make sure your fingers skim their genitals, adding a super sexy teasing sensation.

You can also try some 'sexy pinching' – but do this carefully. While touching during foreplay gradually introduce a pinching action. Pay attention to their responses making sure they're enjoying what might be a new sensation. Don't pinch directly on highly sensitive erogenous zones like the nipples, clitoris or penis. The best places for pinching are the edges of these zones. Unless your partner likes a bit of pain – more on kinky things in the next chapter.

Always start with a gentle pinch, gradually building the tension between your thumb and forefinger. When you move closer to their erogenous zones begin by rubbing your fingers back and forth over the area then gently add in the pinching. For example, if you're going to pinch the fleshy mound of their pubic area, stroke it and then pinch a few times, then repeat the stroking, followed by more pinching.

Move your thumb and forefinger to her pubic mound. First run your fingers back and forth over it a couple times. Then gently pinch the fleshy mound in the centre of the pubic bone. Repeat this, using the pinching action to gently pull up the flesh of the pubic mound. Keep repeating this in a rhythmic action and her clitoris will be stimulated in the most erotic way.

Steamy Sex Tips

Build and keep a rhythmic action going. This will increase blood flow to your partner's genitals, making them feel super aroused. At this point ask them what's feeling best and whether they want you to continue alternating the pinching and stroking, or prefer one or the other.

Practise all of these touching techniques on yourself first, to get an idea of how they might feel to your partner.

One thing that will take your foreplay and sexual satisfaction that bit further is using luscious lubricants, which Tom asked about.

Q Tom: Slippery issue

It may sound silly but I don't really know what to do with lubricants. Please help.

A I'm always glad when people ask me about lubricants because I think people miss out on this easy way to heighten their sexual experience. Never underestimate the power of using luscious lubricants to enhance your sensitivity. There are many lubricants available at good chemists, adult shops and on the internet. They smooth the way for your sexual experience and add a touch of 'raunchy factor'.

Of course you can use lubricants anywhere on the body, but if you're using condoms make sure it's a condom-friendly lubricant. Always be generous with it and warm it between your hands before gently sliding it over your partner's body. An extra sexy use for a lubricant is right over your partner's genitals – for a female partner slide it down her labia, over her perineum and up between her buttocks.

To give her an extra special sensation, have her relax back while you massage her vagina and labia with a big dollop of lubricant on the palm of your hand. Use gentle, but big, sweeping strokes. Ask her to raise her hips slightly and you can really take charge of things and reach right under her bottom and stroke it with a great big, luscious sweeping action from her buttocks right back up over her labia, over her clitoris and onto her pubic mound and lower tummy.

Keep reapplying more lubricant as you need it, and continue this big sweeping action until she can't take any more. By the time you've repeated that a number of times (mind you don't catch her clitoris on the way up with the palm of your hand as she gets aroused), she'll be feeling fantastic. Continue enjoying a luscious lubricant you've chosen throughout sex play and during penetration.

Steamy Sex Tips

Ask her to sit up and cup her breasts as you drizzle some lubricant between them. She can either put on a bit of a show and rub it in while you watch, or you can do that slowly and sensually really bringing her up to fever pitch.

Try some of the lickable, edible lubricants so you can enjoy the full kissing, licking and sucking while enjoying the lubricant action.

Steamy SOS for smooching

You might think kissing is so straightforward that you wonder why I include it in techniques – you'd be very wrong. Research shows a simple kiss can either seal-the-deal on a new relationship, or put someone right off. Zach wanted to kiss to impress.

Q Zach: The Kissing X factor

I'm desperate for a couple of hot kissing techniques to impress my new girlfriend.

A Here are a couple of classic kisses, sure to be appreciated. Begin with the 'Eastern Swirl and Poke' which is fabulous for the lips, but also for teasing the skin on different erogenous zones. Legend has it that this was the 'kiss of choice' for great lovers of the East. Said to arouse a lover's passion you can create some pretty fantastic sensations by moving back and forth between the swirling action and the poking action.

Think of the beginning of this kiss like a French kiss, where you move your tongue inside their mouth and gently swirl it around their tongue. No 'plunging' action. This is a gentle swirl. Next gently poke the inside of their mouth, and around their tongue, with the tip of your tongue. And as its name suggests, you start alternating between swirling and poking – giving them lots of tingling sensations.

 ### Steamy Sex Tips

Impress with this kiss by using it to stimulate your partner's body. Use the 'Eastern Swirl and Poke' down their neck and over their nipples. Swirl the tip of your tongue around their nipples' areola (sensitive in men too.) and then subtly and gently poke their now-erect nipple. Alternate these two sensations and it's highly erotic.

But get ready for more as you move on down their body to their stomach and swirl your tongue around and around the edge of the delicate skin of the belly button. You can then gently poke your tongue into it – a much neglected erogenous zone. Flip your partner onto their stomach and use the 'Swirl and Poke' technique as you trace a line down their back and finish the kiss by swirling your tongue on the cleft of their buttocks.

Steamy sex tip for foot fetishists – when they're straight out of a bath or shower – so their feet are clean – gently swirl and poke around their toes. This can give an amazing sensation, even if you have no interest in feet.

Another wonderful technique is the 'Naughty Dog Kiss' – fantastic for stimulating large erogenous zones. For instance, it's perfect for using on her breasts during foreplay. Your tongue needs to be relaxed – imagine a dog panting on a hot summer's day – that super-relaxed tongue. Start at the base of her breast with a big 'lapping' sweep of your tongue finishing on the tip of her nipple with a gentle flick. Repeat this action, moving around the base of her breast placing your tongue further along this erogenous zone with each lap. This arouses the nerve endings in her skin in this area.

Use the 'Naughty Dog Kiss' along their neck, inner thigh, abdomen and bottom. Get extra sexy and make sure the lapping action just touches the side of her labia/his testicles with your mouth and tongue – quite a sensation. You're not giving oral stimulation at this point, but they'll probably be begging for it.

Classic kissing tips

As with all sets of tips, some seem quite obvious – but they may be obvious to you, but not others.

- Ensure your teeth are clean and your breath's fresh and that the person you're with *wants* to be kissed.

- It's all right if you've *both* been eating garlicky/spicy food, but not if only you have. If you don't have a toothbrush handy then suck a mint before kissing.

- Start slowly and carefully – definitely don't lunge at your partner. Interestingly a large survey found that 56% of people think men should take the lead with kissing – but that's up to you.

- A certain amount of 'wetness' in your mouth is sexy, but make sure you don't get too much saliva into their mouth.

- Relax, loosening your lips so they don't feel rigid to the touch. Only 9% of women report that a firm pressure improves a kiss.

- If they're enjoying your kiss then keep it going. A long, extended kiss is a big turn on.

- Take a break if your mouth gets tired. During this pause simply nuzzle their neck gently.

- Try stroking their lips gently with the tips of your fingers. A light touch can be highly erotic.

- Finally, as you enter a long-term relationship, keep the kissing going. Women in particular often complain that kissing starts to dwindle. You can maintain your sexual and emotional intimacy with lots of luscious kissing lip-action.

Pole positions for your sex life

Sexology research shows that couples tend to settle into two – and sometimes only one – favourite sex position. Although some people are content with this, many couples aren't. Amanda was concerned with this.

Q Amanda: Mixing it up

I love my husband, but I get a bit fed up because we always have sex in either the missionary or spoons position. Can you suggest a position or two that I could throw in the mix that wouldn't be threatening to him?

A I'm always glad to hear when someone is sensitive to their

partner's feelings. When you're not, you're likely to suggest something in a way that tells them you've been bored to tears. Yes, definitely some classic positions like doggy style and strip search (see below) would be easy to add in. From a position like spoons (on your sides, him behind and facing your back) you could quite easily move into doggy. From your side simply move onto your hands and knees, and ask him to move behind you, onto his knees.

Steamy Sex Tips

While in doggy he can reach around her hips and very gently stroke her clitoris as they move together. He can suggest she uses a vibrator gently on herself as he thrusts in this position. She can use the vibrator along her pubic mound, around her clitoral region, over her labia and around the base of his penis as he continues to move carefully. If they don't use a vibrator than she can still stroke herself as his thrusting gains momentum in this position.

For women who like a little bit of 'slap and tickle', doggy style's perfect for him to gently slap her buttocks as he thrusts.

A position that many couples would think is quite difficult but actually isn't, is strip search. This is simply a standing up variation of spoons. She leans against a wall and he holds her from behind, bending his knees in order to enter her, and once inside he can start thrusting. Always start slowly when in a new position, particularly a standing up one, so that you both can find your equilibrium and balance.

Sometimes worrying about the positions you use is *not* about boredom, but more about concern for your partner's full satisfaction. Michael wanted to make sure his partner reached climax.

Q Michael: Pleasure guaranteed?

What is a unique position that's guaranteed to bring a woman to orgasm?

A The best position for the majority of women to climax in is the CAT – the coital alignment technique. This is where she's on top of you in a reverse missionary position, with her legs inside of your legs. She then eases upwards a centimetre or two so that her clitoral region touches your pubic bone. This creates more tension between your pubic bones and also with your penis and her vagina.

Next it's fantastic to give her 'permission' to control the speed, pressure and movement of thrusting. Most women will climax fairly quickly in the CAT if they feel free to 'grind' their clitoral region in a circular, or back and forth, motion against his pubic bone. A man gets a lot of satisfaction from this position too because he'll enjoy her thighs and vagina squeezing his penis tight.

What's absolutely crucial is that she must have absolute freedom to let go and do exactly what feels right to her. When that happens this can be the one position that women, who find it hard to orgasm, will actually orgasm in. Where there's been any difficulty for her in climaxing a fantastic strategy to use is to start in the CAT position and stay there until she climaxes, and then move into his favourite position.

 Steamy Sex Tip

While she's in this position reach around her hips with your fingertips and gently caress her perineum and the back part of her labia. This can give her even more powerful orgasms, particularly if you use a rhythmic, caressing action.

Developing steamy oral sex techniques

Before we look at some specific 'his' and 'hers' type, oral sex questions here are my top tips for being oral-already.

- Ensure you're nice and fresh down there. If you've just showered or bathed, that's the perfect time to encourage oral pleasure. Let's face it if you've been running around all day and then end up in bed together, you won't be fresh smelling or tasting. Beware as women who over-wash or douche with shower gels and/or vaginal washes sometimes end up smelling because they change the normal pH balance of their vagina. Consult your doctor if you end up with any irritation or smell despite being clean because you regularly shower.

- Turn it into foreplay and have a sexy shower or bath together and sensually soap each other down. Don't forget women in particular have a delicate pH balance in the vagina, so don't use lots of soap/shower gel if she's not used to it.

◊◊ Carefully trim your pubic hair so you're likely to keep smelling fresh and it's easier for your partner to give you oral sex. No point in them having to fight their way through a pubic jungle.

◊◊ Your tongue is a muscle and it needs to get in shape with some exercise. Flutter it around, whirl it in a circular motion and generally loosen it. Do this on a daily basis.

◊◊ When giving oral pleasure you're likely to use your hands too. You might grip the shaft of his penis while you suck his glans. Or you might touch her labia while you lick and tease around her clitoris. So make sure your nails are filed and your hands are clean.

◊◊ If you expect to be given oral sex, then you need to give it too. Many women complain their lover wants oral sex but doesn't necessarily want to return the favour. When it comes to good bedroom manners, you should give back what you get.

◊◊ As your partner might be anxious about oral sex, choose a moment to encourage it. A good moment might be during foreplay and as you kiss them gently down their stomach ask if they'd like you to go further.

◊◊ Once you've asked this, keep asking what feels good and what they'd like you to do.

◊◊ Listen to what they say carefully. People have very distinct needs particularly when it comes to making oral sex a pleasurable experience.

◊◊ Some women might take issue with a man ejaculating in their mouth. Set the boundaries and let them know what you do and don't want to do. It might be a woman is happy to give oral pleasure but will remove his penis when it's time for him to orgasm. A man should always give warning when he's reaching that point.

꙳ Never feel pressured into giving/receiving oral sex if you really don't like it. A compromise might be to lavish a few kisses around a partner's genitals while you fondle them and maybe bring them to climax with a hand job.

꙳ Always practise safe sex with a new partner, and that means slipping a condom over him (that's why they have flavours.) or a dental dam/clingfilm over her vagina before giving oral pleasure.

Outstanding oral sex techniques for her

When it comes to giving great cunnilingus, the very first thing I want to say is that a 'stiff upper lip' so to speak is definitely a no-no. Although a 'hard' tongue and lips might benefit the latter stages for *some* women, the majority of women like men to start with a relaxed lip-action. So always think in terms of relaxed lips and a gentle lapping tongue.

However, as a woman's sexual tension builds towards climax, many enjoy it when a man starts to use a 'pouting' type of action that stiffens his lips. The most important thing any partner can do is to *ask her* once you're down there whether she wants a soft, gentle approach or a man with a 'stiff upper lip'. Whatever you do, make sure that you've shaved as you don't want to give her stubble burn. And if facial hair is part of your normal look then be aware of how it might feel to her most tender parts – gently rub your lips and chin on the inside of your wrist to get a vague idea of what she might feel.

Many men don't know what to do with their hands while their mouth is giving her some hot oral-action. Ben asked this very question.

Q Ben: Handy hints

I'm not the most confident lover and wonder what I can do with my hands to enhance my girlfriend's pleasure when I go down on her?

A This question brings me nicely to a wonderful way to arouse her labial area and make sure her labia swell with desire while you're kissing her clitoral region – the 'Lovely Labial Massage' (LLM). A man can really take charge of her pleasure during oral sex with this. Even if you're the most sensitive guy, and you two have the most sensitive and loving relationship, by far the majority of women love it when a man takes charge at different points during sex – particularly oral sex when both people might feel a bit nervous, especially in the early phases of a sexual relationship.

Imagine you two have been caressing each other and things are getting exciting. Ask her to lie back and part her legs. Make sure your hands are nice and warm and your fingertips are covered with a luscious lubricant. As you begin to kiss her clitoral region you can give her a LLM in one of two ways. The first way is to lie 'across' her pelvis with your mouth at her pubic mound, rather than between her legs. Then use the finger tips from one hand beginning from the base of her labia and ever so gently massaging up to the top of one side near her clitoris. Your finger tips can meet your lips at this point. Then move your hand back towards the base of her other side and then repeat, again gently massaging up to the top of that side.

 ### Steamy Sex Tips

The second and super hot way of doing the LLM is kneeling between her legs (again with your mouth gently teasing her clitoral region) and using your hands separately on each of her labia - again starting at the base and gently wiggling your fingers in a massaging motion as you move up her labia to her clitoris. Here again it meets your lips to give her extra stimulation.

There are two key things to heightening her pleasure during a labial massage. First, you need to keep asking her if you're getting the pressure and firmness right.

Because she's getting stimulation from both your lips and your finger tips it's important to check. She might want a more gentle massage or a firmer finger tip massage. Second, you need to keep your fingers well lubricated so they feel heavenly on her labia as your tongue/lips play back and forth over her clitoris.

We are all different when it comes to our particular needs and desires, and some women like a lot of stimulation. Joseph was concerned that he satisfied his wife's needs.

Q Joseph: Keeping the honeymoon feeling

My wife and I have been married for only a year and we're still in that exciting honeymoon phase. My worry is that she likes a lot of physical stimulation and I'd like a great technique to satisfy her.

A A perfect technique for women that like lots of physical touch is 'The Full Four'. This involves your hands exploring the whole area of her vagina and perineum. And this technique is easy to do, and yet so effective in turning her on. To get started allow all four of your finger tips to gently relax over her pubic bone, with your thumb relaxing against her inner thigh and the edge of her pubic mound. Your finger tips should be touching/resting against her labia and introitus (the opening to her vagina).

Ensuring you use a delicate touch, start moving your finger tips up and down her labia. They should be well lubricated with a good-quality lubricant. After a number of strokes start to gently circle your finger tips – again over this whole area. As she begins to get aroused and lubricated you can go back to the rocking, stroking motion and then allow one or two of your finger tips to slide into her vagina. Once one or two of your finger tips are in her vagina, and the other finger tips are still touching her labia, continue the rocking motion. The fact that your whole masculine hand is gently rocking and circulating this area is a huge turn on.

Steamy Sex Tips

Now for the *pièce de résistance*: start to kiss and lick her clitoral region. If at first you find it difficult to coordinate your hands and your mouth, then relax your hands while you stimulate her orally. Then go back to using your hands in the 'Full Four' technique. You can alternate these sensations or eventually coordinate them.

Start easing off from the full technique and gently run your finger tips up and down her vagina and labia as you continue to lick and kiss her. By this time she'll be more than ready for you to start penetration.

It's easy to get into difficulties when you two misread how much the other wants to give oral pleasure – or are resistant to giving it. David had run into some trouble with his girlfriend.

Q David: Going down in popularity

I've never been keen about giving oral sex although to be fair I don't really expect it much myself in return. But my girlfriend has complained that she feels she has to coerce me into it. I love her so much and would like to get around this and show her I'll be more enthusiastic in future.

A The easy solution is to definitely head 'down south' when she least expects it – even before you get down to proper foreplay, after maybe a little bit of kissing. When she realises you're diving headfirst into giving her pleasure, she'll love it because it shows you're not completely selfish – and want to start giving oral pleasure.

Many women feel that the only reason he goes down on her is because he wants the favour returned. By showing her that completely out-of-the-blue you're happy to spoil her, makes her feel you're doing it for her pleasure and not ultimately your own. Doing this also penetrates deep into her subconscious feelings that you find her irresistible 'down below' – or at least you've learned to find her irresistible if you've previously been resisting oral sex.

Steamy Sex Tips

If when giving someone oral sex 'taste' has been an issue, why not smother your partner in your favourite taste treat like chocolate sauce, fruit yoghurt or honey (anything that doesn't irritate the delicate skin of your lover's genitals). Then you can lick a little bit of it off as a compromise. Remember that the way you taste is affected by what you've eaten, e.g. spicy and salty foods are definite culprits in altering the flavour of your natural juices.

Give some 'oral feedback' of a different type – by saying how much you really want to please her this way. A little bit of enthusiasm can go a long way.

Outstanding oral sex techniques for him

As with most of my advice it often works for both male and female partners. However, here are a few typical questions women have asked me about how to pleasure a man orally. Gina simply wanted to know how to get started.

 Gina: Oral advice

I've never given oral sex to a man and now that I'm in a serious relationship how do I get started?

A It's far easier to indulge your lover in oral pleasure than you might think. You can come across as an oral sex 'guru' simply by altering slightly what you do with your mouth – changing the sensations you give him quite dramatically.

Always, always, always take your time and leisurely experiment beginning with kissing his genitals in a sensual way. Begin with soft kisses that aren't directly on his genitals. Some men, though, find very gentle kissing slightly annoying so try different pressures with your lips to see what he responds to. Next you can move on to licking. The way you use your tongue is imagining you're licking a lollipop, gently – an excellent way to start. You can use such licking strokes from the base of his penile shaft up to his glans – the head of his penis. If you want to, also gently lick his perineum – the area between his thighs at the back of his testicles.

Next move on to lapping – this time imagining you're lapping a luscious ice-cream cone. In essence it's a bigger version of licking. Allow your mouth to relax and lap with a completely relaxed tongue. Once he's aroused use these lapping strokes around his testicles and again up and down his penis.

Steamy Sex Tips

An extra little technique to try – something most people wouldn't think to use – is a rubbing action with your lips as opposed to a kissing action. Relax your lips, and rub them back and forth or in circular motions around the shaft and base of his penis. Then gently rub your very moist lips against the end of his penis. But make sure you moisten them so they slip and slide across this sensitive area.

Here's a warning about the 'flicking' technique used in too many porn films – often with men flicking their tongues quickly across a woman's clitoris and women doing the same to the end of a man's penis. In the real world this flicking would be too painful for most people. But if he likes extra stimulation then try giving him a flicking sensation with your tongue. Move it very quickly – practice makes perfect, so here's where those tongue exercises mentioned above come in handy.

Why not alternate flicking with a swirling technique – imagine a swirling whirlpool and try using your tongue this way. You can apply this swirling action with your tongue all around his glans and also down around his testicles.

Sometimes a partner will try and guide you, but it's not always easy if you're feeling anxious at that moment to understand what they want. Sally wasn't sure about sucking her partner.

Q Sally: Top tips for oral sex

I seem to produce a lot of saliva when I try and suck my fiancé's penis. Any tips on a basic sucking technique for oral sex?

A Getting stuck into a sucking action can be a bit tricky. But imagine you're gently sucking a long piece of spaghetti into your mouth. This is the action you want to imitate – that mostly uses your lips and fairly gently at that. Once you've got this technique mastered remember you need to be careful applying a sucking action to the head of a man's penis for too long a time. It can become painful. Keep asking for his guidance as to how long and how much sucking pressure he likes. Definitely try taking one of his testicles in your mouth and gently suck inwards for a different sensation.

If you alternate between all these different techniques, you'll become a confident lover when you're asked to give oral sex.

Steamy Sex Tip

A unique sensation for him, particularly if he likes a gentle touch, is for you to try humming. You may not have a singing voice but you can definitely give him some thrills by humming while you're giving him oral sex. Wrap your lips around his testicles and quietly hum – he'll love the vibrations.

Alanna wanted to know how to take things a bit further when it came to oral sex, having been married for five years and feeling she needed to do something new.

Q Alanna: Oral surprise

How can I surprise my husband of five years by developing my oral sex technique?

A He'll love the 'Worshipping at the Altar' technique. Kneel between his legs while he stands (casually throw a pillow down to kneel on). Hold his hips while you give him oral sex and/or reach around and caress his buttocks if he'll like that sort of stimulation. A word of warning: this might lead to you getting a 'Pearl Necklace' where he climaxes over your neck. Obviously only let him do this if it turns you on.

Alternatively get him into the 'Kneeling Pose' where he kneels over your chest while you lie flat on your back. Holding his testicles in your hands he can then tilt his penis into your mouth. You can control him – so he doesn't get too excited and thrust too hard – by gripping his hips.

Steamy Sex Tips

Why not try 'Picking the Plums', where he kneels on your bed and rests back on his legs which leaves his penis and testicles free for you to caress and play with. You can lie on your back with your head between his thighs. This is a great position to simply lick or suck his testicles while you masturbate him with your hands. Very hot.

≋

Get yourselves into the '69' position so you can give each other oral pleasure at the same time. Lie on your sides facing each other head to toe, so you can access each other. Or one of you can lie on your back and the other arches over you, again head to toe, to enjoy oral sex together.

Miscellaneous and marvellous pleasures and techniques

There are many things that can improve your sex technique and one of the most important ones is not being frightened to try sex toys. I say 'frightened' because some people feel a bit intimidated – particularly men who might feel that their partner prefers a vibrator over them. Believe me, she won't – at least if you are good at giving foreplay and listening to what she wants.

Vibrators come in all shapes and sizes. If you're not feeling very experimental, and haven't used vibrators, you should simply go for one of the basic penis-shaped vibrators. Even the most basic vibrators usually have speed variations from slow to fast. Before you use a new vibrator get to know how it feels on your own hand. Eric wondered, as many men do, how to get started with a little sex toy experimentation.

Q Eric: Good vibrations?

I'm curious how to use a vibrator on my girlfriend without hurting her?

A Never launch yourself at her with a new vibrator in hand. Always begin with some foreplay, and once you've enjoyed this get out some lubricant and gently cover her lower tummy and pubic mound with it. Next, take the vibrator and start using it in gentle sweeping motions on its lowest (most gentle) setting. Here comes that magic word – *ask* her what feels good.

Steamy Sex Tip

To guarantee she gets incredibly turned on, rather than using the vibrator with the actual end of it touching her skin, lay it almost flat along her pubic bone and start to move it back and forth. This means you cover quite a large area with its vibrations. Vibrating across her pubic mound and lower abdomen in this way will drive her crazy because it stimulates the deeper parts of her 'clitoral arms'.

You can use a sex toy to show each other different sensations that you like. They're fantastic because there's such a range available. Try some standard vibrators, but also those that stimulate the clitoris, the anus, the G spot, etc. Unless he's into it I'd stay away from the massive, vibrating penises that can put men off, and instead go for something sleek and sexy.

Alfresco sex can be great fun. Natasha wondered about taking sex outside with her boyfriend.

Natasha: The great, sexy, outdoors

I don't want my fairly new boyfriend to think I'm a freak because I'd like to have sex outdoors – how should I go about it?

A To get him thinking along the same lines, why not suggest meeting him for lunch in the park and pack a small picnic. Go for fun finger foods to feed each other. But don't just lie around on the grass, instead try something like playing a game of Frisbee because this'll get your blood pumping. Also the competitive nature of playing games helps to boost testosterone levels, which will make you both feel sexy. Once you're feeling that way, start some sexy chat about finding a secluded place to mess around.

Steamy Sex Tips

Be prepared that alfresco sex is often 'quickie' sex. Because of the risk of getting caught (the risk is half the turn on for many couples) you should both be as 'worked up' as possible before you actually go and have sex somewhere secluded. So indulge in some hot-talk about the adventure you're going to have.

Here are a few extra tips to ensure a successful alfresco sex experience: take along a cushion to pad out any tender body part (e.g. your bottom) that may have to press against, say, a stone wall. Bring sun cream for any under-exposed body area that may end up seeing the light of day – like your bottom. Be ready with a cardigan/ sweatshirt to whip on at the sound of a farmer's tractor. A large blanket or beach towel is handy to lie on to protect you from scratchy grass/foliage. If you get carried away when you're not expecting it, stop if you don't have protection with you. Remember it's against the law to have sex in a public place, so be discreet.

Finally there's an added benefit of having sex outside – being in the sun for just 15 minutes increases levels of serotonin, making you both feel good and therefore more inclined to have sex anyway.

Sometimes we overlook the obvious when thinking about little tricks and techniques to get our partner in the mood. Alistair was concerned with this.

Q Alistair: How do I get her in the mood?

I'm not lazy, but I work long hours and I'm not very good at the romantic stuff and would like some suggestions for getting my wife in the mood quickly.

A Lots of things will get her in the mood, have a look at the first couple of chapters, but here are some extra little techniques. To energise her, squeeze her some fresh juice and spoon-feed her a fruit salad. The tangy flavours will stimulate her palate and give her a fresh feeling. Also the vitamins will give her a little extra energy. To get her aroused, take a plump strawberry, cut it in half and gently rub the fresh fruit across her nipple – then lick it off. This is just enough sexiness to make her want you more.

Next give her a genuine compliment. Women can tell when they're being fibbed to, but a genuine compliment will make her feel loving. It'll boost her confidence and feeling more confident will mean she's feeling more confident sexually too. Also try surprising her – go for some fresh milk or the papers and come back with her favourite chocolates or flowers. It shows you're thinking of her even when doing the simplest errand like going to the shop.

Steamy Sex Tips

Stimulate her in sensual ways that you've never tried before and you're likely to get her hot. For example, use SEPs (simple erotic pleasures) and offer to wash her hair and gently swirl your finger tips around her scalp with the warm, sudsy water.

≈

Offer to paint her fingernails and while you do so, gently caress each of her fingers. Such touching techniques will guarantee the production of oxytocin, which is the feel-good hormone that promotes emotional bonding between you. Once she's feeling all warm and sensual towards you, she'll be much more likely to want sex.

Another one of the best ways to get her in the mood is to choose a sex guide or erotic story to read to help spice things up. Remember that women are aroused through their minds.

Then also consider 'location, location, location' – simply varying your sexual technique and rather than going up behind her in the bedroom and doing some of your usual moves, do so in the kitchen, the sitting room, in the bathroom, etc.

Sex Doctor's Conclusions

We've covered lots of different techniques you can try to spice things up in your sex life. Technique varies tremendously from person to person and the way one person does something as simple as stroking their partner's nipples will be done differently by another. Always remember that the sorts of techniques a previous partner liked may not work with your next partner. Most of the fun is in finding out how much you enjoy using a technique, and how much they like it – or if you like having it used on you. Feel free to sex-periment in different ways with the techniques I've described making them your own. But now I want to turn up the heat and look at some quirks and kinks when it comes to sex.

Chapter 6
Quirky and kinky sex

15% of people report they get turned on by spanking

8% of people say they get aroused dressing up in uniforms

People have all sorts of quirks and kinks when it comes to their sexual desires and interests, many of which they keep secret – at least until they build trust with their sexual partner. But because of this secrecy many people start to feel guilty or that there's something wrong with them, and it can become a negative cycle affecting the way they relate to a partner.

As far as I'm concerned what you get up to in your bedroom, as consenting adults, is your business – obviously as long as it's legal. I already discussed communication techniques in Chapter 4. And using good communication is crucial when it comes to your own personal quirks and kinks – and trying to enlist your partner to try them.

It's impossible in one chapter to cover every possible sexual kink, fetish and thrill, so I'm tackling a selection of the ones that people experience relatively frequently.

Let's begin with your fantasy life. Henry was concerned about the fantasy his wife confessed to him. Before we get to Henry's question, let me point out the benefits of an active fantasy life:

A healthy fantasy life can benefit you because:

◊◊ You can enjoy fantasy chat for its own sake - it can be fun.

§ Fantasies help you escape sexual boredom.

§ Sharing your fantasy with your partner can turn them on too.

§ By encouraging your partner to share theirs with you, you double the possibilities for fantasy scenarios.

§ When you're separated from your partner – or you're single and enjoying some self-pleasure – your active fantasy life adds to your pleasure.

§ You can fantasise about exciting places and be with sexy people you'd never be with in real life.

§ Fantasising can give you fresh ideas to actually try out.

§ Fantasising is free.

Q Henry: Shocking fantasies

My wife and I have a good sex life (after three years and still going strong) and started chatting about our fantasies the other day. I didn't say anything at the time but was fairly shocked to hear she fantasises about being a porn star. Is this something I should worry about?

A Let me reassure you this shouldn't worry you in the slightest, as many women wonder what it would be like to star in a porn film. Such a fantasy theme covers many potential levels when it comes to sexual curiosity such as wanting to be desired by the people who watch the film, to revelling in the sexual skills. The earthiness of this fantasy also helps the average woman to feel she can get a bit 'down and dirty' rather than always being a 'good girl' in bed.

Steamy Sex Tips

Why not take some hot photographs of each other in different porn-star-like poses? When you're feeling confident you could film yourselves. It can be super-hot watching yourselves in the throes of passion. Also you can get really 'dirty' when you talk to each other, because it's only a fantasy after all.

Keep encouraging the fantasy talk, as it will keep things spicy. Don't forget if you film yourselves to be aware of lighting and angles. You won't find it sexy if you film yourselves from an angle that makes your bottoms appear huge or something like that – unless of course that's your kink. You can always do some test shots to check out the angles you're going to film from.

Before you start making your own porn, agree that your films are to be kept under lock and key. For anyone in a rocky relationship I'd think twice about doing this as you don't want to have a break-up and find out your 'home video' ends up on the internet, posted there by your angry ex.

Common female fantasy themes:

〴 **Group sex** – a common fantasy theme for women. Often the most unadventurous woman will surprise her partner by fantasising about group sex. The heart of this fantasy is about abandoning caution and 'normal' behaviour.

〴 **Lesbian/bi-sexual fantasies** – Same-sex fantasy scenarios are common, with most women fantasising about this at some point. Such fantasies often involve seeing how different it would be to experience a woman's body and touch compared to a man's.

🔥 **Sex with a stranger -** It might seem shocking to some that women might fantasise about stranger sex involving no-strings thrills. But it's a popular fantasy theme. Such fantasies allow women to enter a traditionally sexual 'no-go' area.

🔥 **Sex with some sort of service provider like a repair or delivery man, doctor, etc. -** Such fantasies play on our many common stereotypes that the men who provide services for us will also provide a sexy service. Common fantasies are along the lines of, e.g., a damsel-in-distress who calls a plumber for help. He turns out to be gorgeous and she has brazen sex with him on the kitchen floor.

🔥 **Exotic sex: being swept off to a foreign country against your will and being kept as a captive sex slave -** These are common fantasy themes that free up women from sexual inhibitions. Because the fantasies revolve around being taken against their will, then it frees the woman from being responsible for the sex. Obviously let me stress that such fantasies have nothing to do with actually being taken against their will in real life – that is *not* what a woman wants.

🔥 **Sex with a celebrity -** Such fantasies are pure escapism and usually involve a woman's favourite movie or pop star. The ultimate celebrity fantasy is where the woman becomes the object of the celebrity's desire.

🔥 **Being secretly spied upon -** Such fantasy scenarios play into women's desires to be seen to be desirable. As well as playing into themes of flaunting their body in front of someone.

🔥 **The 'casting couch' -** Many women fantasise about having to give sexual favours in return for some sort of a perk like a pay rise. Mixing the themes of 'work' and sexual activity explores sexually exciting themes of power in workplace relationships.

🔥 **Domination and bondage, discipline and sadomasochism -** Again, exploring themes/taboos around domination, power, etc., through the safety of fantasies can be very erotic. Think of the powerful erotic tension in the film *The Secretary* and you'll understand how themes of power can become the stuff of fantasies.

≬ **High-risk sex where there's a chance of discovery** – Risky sex is a popular theme with many women because many don't take risks in their sex lives. Fantasising about joining the 'mile high club', or having a quickie in the office behind the stationery cupboard, or even in the toilet in a bar, etc., explore the thrills of potentially being caught out.

One important point about sharing your fantasies with a partner was raised by Angela's question.

Q **Angela: Am I enough for my boyfriend?**
I was really hurt when my boyfriend started describing this fantasy he has about a threesome with me and another woman. It wasn't that he had any specific women in mind, but got turned on generally by the idea of a threesome and it makes me wonder if I'm not enough for him?

A Because this is a very common complaint – a partner feeling offended/threatened by what their partner fantasises about – I'd like to spell out the good manners of sharing your fantasies.

Basic bedroom etiquette:

≬ Timing's crucial. If your partner's just confessed undying love for you and/or made some big gesture to you, that's not the right time to tell them you have a fantasy about having rampant sex with a stranger you meet on holiday.

⚠ If the timing feels right to share some sexy fantasy talk, then begin by sounding them out. When you're cuddling say something like, 'You're so hot looking I've fantasised you're my boss and I'll do anything you ask because I've got such a crush.' Taking this approach makes a fantasy sound alluring rather than threatening.

⚠ Next, you can ask if they've got any secret fantasy they'd like to share. Tell them how much you'd love to hear what they think about. Give them the confidence to say what they want about their fantasy life.

⚠ Whatever your fantasy, always put your partner in the middle of it. Unless it's something where they wouldn't play a part like you fantasising about doing a dance in a crowded lap-dancing bar. But otherwise you have to put your partner into it or you risk hurting them or turning them off.

⚠ As the saying goes, variety is the spice of life, so make sure you explore different fantasy scenarios. If you repeatedly tell them the same scenarios, say, that you watch your partner have sex with someone else, they might start feeling threatened by this. You can see how they'd begin to think that you only get turned on by the idea of watching them have sex with someone.

⚠ Honesty is the right policy, but this has to be with tact when sharing your fantasies. Complete honesty, e.g. where you tell them in detail about your fantasy about your next-door neighbour will be hurtful. However, change such a fantasy into your neighbour fantasising about you two in bed, then it has a different feel to it.

⚠ Even if your partner wants you to 'go first', always then ask them to describe their fantasies. Otherwise if one of you is more dominant or has a particularly active imagination it's easy to dominate these conversations.

〰 Beware that what you might think of as a sexy fantasy, your partner might find a big turn off. A bit of common sense means you're less likely to shock your partner. Toning down something that might be considered a bit wild is the best way to start.

〰 I'm sure I don't have to tell you that some fantasies shouldn't be turned into reality. Often the reality is sadly disappointing whereas keeping up the hot fantasy chat hopefully won't get you into trouble.

〰 It's a fact that some people simply won't get involved in fantasy chat. It's simply a no-go zone for them. You might just have to accept this in your relationship. Although hopefully some very gentle fantasy chat like, 'I've fantasised about you wearing old-fashioned stockings and suspenders', will be acceptable.

By far the majority of men fantasise, but that doesn't mean that they aren't shy or concerned about opening up. Stella wanted her long-term partner to open up about his.

Q **Stella: How can I get him to share his fantasies?**
I'm sure my partner fantasises but he's very shy about expressing himself in bed. Any suggestions?

A There's often a crossover between male and female fantasies, so ask if one of yours turns him on. But sometimes the best solution in this case is to simply start running some classic fantasy scenarios past your partner and ask if any turns them on.

Here are some classic male fantasy themes:

〰 **Voyeuristic fantasies –** Many men have voyeuristic fantasies where they watch, say, their neighbour strip off and get into her shower. Or they watch another couple have sex – this may explain the popularity of 'dogging' where people seek out other like-minded people to have sex in front of. Usually this takes place parked up in a fairly secluded setting.

〰️ **Sex with forbidden people like nuns, nannies and school teachers** – Men quite commonly fantasise about forbidden figures including ultimate forbidden figures like nuns. These things elicit feelings of risk and excitement in a fantasy scenario.

〰️ **Sex with prostitutes** – Even men who don't use prostitutes often fantasise about paying for sex. Such themes allow them to cross into the territory of dirty sex where they can ask what they want for. For some men this is about escapism and uncomplicated sex without strings.

〰️ **Being seduced by a forbidden person that you know** – Some classic male fantasies revolve around a forbidden woman that they know like a girlfriend's mother, their wife's best friend, etc. Such themes are about enjoying forbidden fruit on your doorstep and the risk that would go with this.

〰️ **Watching lesbian sex** – The majority of straight men fantasise about women having sex together. There are many levels to this – like how two women turn each other on and also fantasising that they'll be invited to join the action.

〰️ **Bondage, domination and sadomasochism** – Men often fantasise about BDSM – from very different perspectives. For some men they want to let go and take a more submissive role and be dominated by the partner in their fantasies. And for other men they get aroused thinking about dominating their partner.

〰️ **Group and three-way sex** – Many men have a less inhibited view of group sex and get turned on fantasising about 'faceless' sex with a variety of people. One common theme is proving themselves to be fantastic lovers to lots of different people.

- ◊◊ **Being a successful businessman** – Having power and using it to seduce people is a common fantasy theme for men. The thrill of abusing their power is a huge turn on. Often these fantasies spill into risky sex around the photocopier, in the staff toilet, etc.

- ◊◊ **Being seduced by a sexy nurse** – This common fantasy appeals to men who want to be looked after and allow someone to take charge of their sexual satisfaction.

- ◊◊ **Watching his partner being taken by another man** – Another voyeuristic fantasy theme that's common in men who are aroused by the idea of watching another man take their partner. Often the theme underlying such fantasies is about the competition involved where their fantasy continues down the path where their partner says that he's better than the stranger she's just had sex with.

- ◊◊ **Gay sex encounter** – Many men have fantasies about gay sex experiences although they don't always want to admit it. When they discuss such fantasies in confidence, it's often simple sexual curiosity rather than a real longing to live life as a gay man.

- ◊◊ **Having sex with a pregnant woman** – A common fantasy theme with men is having sex with a pregnant woman whose ripe breasts and lush stomach arouses them.

- ◊◊ **Being a police/prison officer that takes a beautiful prisoner** – The themes of such fantasies are often about power and control. It's also the excitement about abusing their position to take advantage of someone who doesn't have a choice.

- ◊◊ **Anal sex** – As many women aren't interested in anal sex this is still fairly taboo. Of course, any sex that's taboo is like showing a red rag to a bull.

Taking the next step – role-play

Often a logical step when people start sharing their fantasies is to try a little bit of role-play. It's understandable that some people might feel threatened, wondering what on earth role-play involves. First off, role-play doesn't have to involve fancy costumes and imaginative settings. It can be incredibly simple but still a good way to spice things up, as Geoff wanted to.

Q **Geoff: Role-play tips?**

I think my partner would be up for trying some role-play in our sex life but I haven't a clue where to start. Also she's fairly shy about suggesting new things. We have discussed our sexual fantasies together.

A You're a good part of the way there if you've discussed sexual fantasies. Role-play is simply about taking these a step further and bringing them to life. Couples can find role-playing one of their fantasies very 'releasing'. It means that instead of being 'themselves' they get to play a role and so feel less inhibited. Pretending to be someone else definitely helps you shed sexual inhibitions. They can always excuse whatever they do (or ask for) in the role-play as being down to the role and not their 'real self'.

Steamy Sex Tips

A couple of hot but simple role-plays include 'strangers in the night', where you two agree to meet up at a bar and pretend to be strangers who chat each other up and tumble into bed for an illicit night of hot sex. And another easy one is you knock on the door pretending to be the handsome neighbour who needs to borrow something. But you end up seducing your partner in the kitchen with lots of flirting and dirty chat.

It's easy to get started once you've mentioned to your partner you'd like to try role-play. Check out what you've already got in your bedroom that might add to the sex-perience. Once you get into it you might even decide to visit a hire shop to hire an outfit – like a uniform – to wear. Adult shops, even on the high street, usually have lots of role-play outfits, including classic ones like a French maid outfit.

Here are some extra 'rules' of role-play:

- Best to have a fantasy in mind before you introduce the idea of doing a role-play. Have a look at the advice about fantasy etiquette above on how to introduce the idea.

- If experimenting with role-play doesn't go to plan, it's best to keep 'costumes' and other such items to a minimum. No point in spending a small fortune on costumes and accessories, only to find you don't enjoy role-play.

- Obviously if your partner is not interested then don't keep pressurising them to try some role-play – some people just don't find it appealing.

- Definitely don't do any role-play that lands you in trouble with the law in any way.

- In your role-play, don't use things from around the home that aren't meant to be sex toys – like glass bottles inserted into the vagina, etc., when you're pretending to be a vineyard owner seducing a visitor.

- As with any sex play that involves a fantasy scenario, be aware that it doesn't become an obsession - so don't allow role-play to take over your sex life. I've met some people that have become so obsessed with a particular role-play that they never have simple, loving sex. Ultimately either one of them might start feeling they're not in touch with each other any more in a real way as the role-play dominates their sex play.

Steamy Sex Tip

One final hot suggestion for a bit of fantasy role-play – why not choose some old (but clean and neat.) stockings and a dress or top. Ask your partner to rip them off in the height of passion just like an old-fashioned bodice-ripper. Turn it into a fun fantasy that he's a pirate and he's captured her, the fair maiden, then rips open her dress. Or he can pretend to be the dominant office manager who calls her in for a 'dressing down' and then literally gives her a dressing down by ripping off her skirt and ravishing her.

How fetishes fit into your sex life

People ask me about fetishes all the time, and to begin with many don't really understand what a fetish is – although they may not want to let their partner know that – as with Jenny.

Q Jenny: Mystery fetishes

I feel so foolish asking but my new boyfriend says he has a fetish he'll tell me about when we get to know each other better. But just what is a fetish?

A You're smart to ask because many get confused by the word fetish, and for good reason. The word fetish has entered everyday language and is used loosely to describe something you find a turn on that is necessary to some degree for your sexual satisfaction. For example, a man might say, 'I get turned on by a woman in PVC', but in reality he may or may not also be turned on by a woman who isn't wearing it. But in the true spirit of a fetish, it would mean he *wouldn't* get turned on unless a woman was wearing PVC. Or if he was good at fantasising about PVC, then he could get sexually satisfied during sex if he imagined her decked out in it from head to toe. In psychological terms, a true fetish requires the fetish object (or thoughts of it) to be present for the person to achieve sexual arousal.

Fetishes can range from the completely harmless, like men who love women with big breasts and seek out sexual partners endowed with these, to what most people would find bizarre or downright disgusting. When someone has a fetish for something like scat-play – or coprophilia (sexual arousal by faeces) – the rest of us wonder quite rightly how on earth they could develop such an interest.

With careful exploration, you can usually uncover the reasons why an extreme or revolting fetish develops. At an anecdotal level I've discussed with many people why their fetishes have arisen, and it can be an interesting process. Let me simplify what can be a complex process. A fetish may begin when some sort of sexual arousal occurs in the presence of either a sexually related – or an *unrelated* – stimulus. When it comes to a related stimulus, let's say a man has his first sexual experience with a woman with large breasts – he might then come to be very turned on only by large breasts.

When it comes to an 'unrelated' stimulus, let me use an example someone once gave me: a man had quick and exciting sex with a friend's girlfriend who happened to be wearing fluffy slippers. She was bent over the bed and he took her from behind getting a good view of those slippers throughout the whole sexual encounter. After that he came to associate fluffy slippers with raunchy and exciting sex. So thinking about this example you can see how an unrelated stimulus goes on to become sexually charged.

Other times the development of an extreme fetish like coprophilia that would disgust most adults comes from a quite complex process when sexual arousal is related to excitement or risk. So, say, a child might have made a mess in the toilet with his bowel movement and then when he gets told off he feels a thrill of excitement at having been a bit naughty. Such early memories can shape what excites us or feels risky (and then something we want to try.) as adults.

It's undeniable that there's an element of risk or at least excitement in a lot of fetishes. And as our sense of sexuality is formed early in our lives it's easy to see how unusual desires can come from experiences early on. Fetishes can originate later in life, from the pairing of something that becomes sexually charged. Barbara was worried about this.

Q Barbara: Is my fetish normal?

I've always considered myself to have a normal sexual desire, but I must admit that I've developed a bit of a fetish for hairy men. My last boyfriend was very hairy and fantastic in bed. Now I find myself only drawn to men who I can tell are very hairy. Is there something wrong with me?

A No, there is nothing wrong with this except that you might miss out on some darned good lovers who aren't hairy. This is the pitfall of a fetish that completely takes over someone's sexual desires. Yes, by all means appreciate hairy men but do give others – that aren't particularly hirsute – a look-in too.

Some sexy stripping

Fantasy and role-play brings me nicely along to stripping for your partner. I can't tell you how many people wish their partner would strip for them now that lap dancing's on practically every street corner. Jeremy wanted his wife to have a go.

Q Jeremy: Strip tease

I'd absolutely love it if my wife would strip for me. I've hinted about it but haven't actually asked her. I want to maximise the chances she'll say yes.

A Maximising the chance a partner will strip for you takes a whole load of encouragement and confidence boosting – so get ready to make them feel good about themselves. As well as boosting the way they feel about themselves, you can then start dropping into the conversation how much it would turn you on if they'd do even a few strip moves.

Steamy Sex Tip

If you want your partner to strip, why not put on a bit of a show for them first? Get the music that you want to move to sorted out and surprise them – even if you do it in a funny way simply to make them laugh.

Steamy stripping guide

Here are lots of tips to get you started on a stripping 'career':

- Practice makes perfect, so when on your own try some 'moves' you feel comfortable with.

- Choose music you feel confident moving to. Whether it's classic mood music, thumping rock or smooth R & B, you have to like it.

- Practise in clothes that come off easily. You'll have more confidence knowing that they'll be easy to get off.

❀ Once you've practised some moves you feel comfortable with, leave the CD in the player ready to go.

❀ When you practise, imagine you're a lap dancer or male stripper. Visualise the sorts of moves they make and add them to your repertoire.

❀ Don't forget to practise teasing your partner by touching yourself as you move.

❀ Think about the hot and flirty things you'd say to your partner when they're watching you.

❀ To create a sexy atmosphere, have some candles ready for soft lighting.

❀ You'll get confidence with slow and sensual moves and not anything too complicated.

❀ When the time is right dim the lights, light the candles, start the CD, and ask your partner to sit in a chair.

❀ Have fun with it – why not tie their hands to the chair so there's no touching?

❀ Get playful and agree some 'rules' like you can fondle and touch them, but they can't touch you.

❀ If you're feeling daring you can do some 'research' for your strip routines by going to watch some lap dancing together.

❀ For extra confidence, go to a strip or a lap dancing class, offered in most cities.

Quirky and kinky sex-play suggestions

People get turned on by all sorts of things – above Barbara was turned on by hirsute men, and here Kathleen was concerned about her boyfriend's interest in hair – or the lack of it.

Q Kathleen: A hairy issue

My new boyfriend has mentioned that he'd like me to shave my pubic hair. This isn't the first time a man has said this – what's up with this?

A Many men appreciate 'shaven-havens'. But what's good for you is also good for him, so why not suggest you both get a little daring and shave each other's pubic hair? Not only will this generate trust between you, but it also deepens intimacy. A word of warning: never shave each other when you've been drinking or taking recreational drugs. Begin by a having a warm, sensual shower. Then take turns to lie back on soft, warm towels for your 'trim'.

Begin by trimming excess pubic hair – particularly on him as men's hair can grow quite long. Then begin the shaving very *gently* – help the process with some sensitive-care, hair conditioner or sensitive skin shaving gel. When it comes to shaving her, he might not be able to get into every little fold of her labia. Tweezing can get rid of any stray hairs. Both of you should enjoy the sense of freedom and extra sensitivity that shaving gives you.

 Steamy Sex Tips

Throw caution to the wind and go for some 69 pleasure once you're both shaved. Take time over pleasuring each other orally. This can be incredibly erotic as you're both going to be feeling super turned on.

≈

If you're annoyed by the itchy regrowth that happens a day or two after shaving, compromise by simply trimming your pubic hair closely. You might want to surprise your partner by going to the salon for a full waxing if you don't want to have your partner trim/shave you. Also at the salon you could have your pubic hair shaped into something fun and sexy – like a heart or a thunderbolt.

Time to get all tied up

Many people are curious about BDSM – bondage and domination, and sadomasochism. It can sound much more frightening than it is, because there are 'vanilla' varieties of these activities, with vanilla meaning gentle or 'light' versions. Mark wanted to know how to get started with this sort of sex-play.

Q Mark: Wanting to get tied down

I'd love it if my wife would agree to some bondage. But I haven't a clue how to get started.

A First, you need to get into your mind that the main element of bondage-play is about teasing. Yes, teasing that involves ties, sashes, ropes, handcuffs and blindfolds, etc., but teasing your partner all the same. Aside from the teasing aspect to bondage-play there are a lot of erotic features like the fantasy and role-play side of things. Many people fantasise about bondage, and those who try it out tend to get started using role-play as the catalyst to a bondage session.

Before you get started you should be warned that some people panic at the mention of bondage-play. They wrongly assume – hopefully your wife won't – that it's going to be heavy sadism and masochism – which it is not. Keep this in mind for when you start talking about experimenting with her – you're best advised to put it in the context of a fantasy you've had.

Steamy Sex Tips

Begin with asking if she'll handcuff you with some of those soft, fur-lined handcuffs available from any adult shop. Make it seem fun and non-threatening. Or if you think she'll be up for it, ask if you can handcuff her, telling her you want to tease her when she can't wriggle free.

Anyone interested in some bondage-play should go on a fun 'shopping trip' with their partner and just get used to looking at things like whips, spanking paddles and all the little accessories that go with B&D and S&M. For example, there are all sorts of nipple/genital clamps available to add a little bit of pain/pleasure to your sex-play. There's a surprising variety of clamps and chains to play with as well as things like 'cock rings' and anal plugs. When you shop together you get an idea of what your partner is and isn't up for.

Some men and women get really hot when, say, their hands are tied/handcuffed together and their knickers/pants pulled down and they're helpless to stop their partner fondling or even spanking them. It can be super steamy knowing you're helpless as your partner has their wicked way with you – bending you over the side of the chair or bed and then teasing or spanking (gently, mind you.) your bare bottom.

Definitely sex-periment once you've tied/handcuffed your partner's wrists together with a bit sex chat, pretending to dominate them. Telling them you're going to have your evil way with them and do whatever you want to do can heighten both of your experiences.

Some people have no interest in things like bondage-play and can't understand why their partner *is* interested in it. Michelle felt like this.

Q Michelle: Pleasure/pain

I've always thought my fiancé was fairly normal but he's recently been hinting that he likes the feeling bondage-play gives to him. Unbelievably he says it helps him 'relax'. What is going on here? And does this mean he wants me to cause him some pain?

A It's easy to get the wrong end of the stick when it comes to what your partner says about bondage. He probably means it allows him some emotional/sexual freedom because he can experiment with different roles. Some people enjoy changing between taking the dominant role, then the submissive role, crossing between the two. Other people like to stick to one of those roles, and very often it's different to the role they have in their relationship or another part of their life – like their working life.

Let me clarify some of these terms, because many people get confused between bondage and dominant/submissive sex-play that are different from sadomasochistic (S&M) practices. Essentially bondage-play involves restraint, control, developing sexual tension, teasing and sometimes giving verbal commands to a partner in order to get them to 'submit' to your demands. S&M is more likely to involve real pain and degradation. That said, people will have their own boundaries and definitions and some lump all such practices together.

Steamy Sex Tip

For a little bit of fun, experimental 'pain', an easy and quite non-threatening way to do this is by getting 'spiky' – give him a cross between some erotic pain and a back massage. Blindfold your partner and get him to lie comfortably on the floor on his stomach. You can pad out the carpet with some soft towels or blankets for him to lie on. Next, test your partner's pain-pleasure zone on his back by gently digging a stiletto heel into it. After testing his pain threshold you might be able to gently and carefully 'walk' on him in a pair of stilettos. Obviously with any such sex-play a partner needs to let you know if something's getting too painful.

Establishing ground rules

Establish ground rules for any BDSM sex-play to keep it safe:

- Agree a code word that's 'neutral' (like 'zebra' or 'flower'), so it can't be misinterpreted. If either of you says the code word, that tells the other that no matter what you're doing, you want to stop. It needs to be neutral as so many things said during the height of passion might be confusing. For instance, it can't be 'No, stop', because sometimes we say no as part of a role-play. If you don't trust your partner to stop when you say the code word, then you shouldn't be doing this sort of sex-play with them.

- Never give in to pressure to do something that frightens you or causes you anxiety. That wouldn't be a turn on. Beware of subtle forms of pressure. The subtlest type of pressure being where you feel you want to please your partner so you give in to a suggestion that you really don't want to try.

- Don't do dangerous things. For instance you might be fascinated by the idea of auto-erotic asphyxiation where people restrict their own airways or get a partner to restrict their airways. My message is simple: *never, ever restrict airways*.

- Don't try BDSM when you've been drinking or taking recreational drugs. This may sound very conservative, but these things lower your inhibitions and your idea of what's safe and not safe changes when under the influence. Drugs and alcohol also alter your pain threshold.

❀ Do not leave your partner unattended. If you've restrained them in any way, untie them if you're leaving the room. It might sound like a joke to try to 'scare' them but accidents can happen.

❀ Know how to tie knots. Practice makes perfect, and it's important if you're thinking about tying up a partner that you know how to undo anything you've tied. I highly recommend tying simple bows. Believe me, it is far from amusing when you're both ready for hot sex and you can't get the restraint off. If something feels uncomfortable it will undoubtedly feel worse later on. Make sure you, and/or your partner, feels comfortable when, say, your hands are tied behind your back.

❀ Tying each other up can be a big turn on, but don't restrain any single area for too long. Particularly when using something like, say, a cock ring it should never be on for more than 20 minutes. And shorter if there's any discomfort.

❀ Know how to keep it clean. Hygiene's important in sex-play that's getting kinky. It's easy to forget about hygiene when, say, you're thinking about tying your partner up and teasing them with a vibrator. So when you've used a sex toy on your restrained lover's vagina, don't then slip it into their anal area – and vice versa. Any sex toy, etc., used in the anal area should be washed before further use. An easy solution is to keep two sex toys to hand with one restricted to anal pleasure and the other for other erogenous zones.

Deciding what will heighten your partner's pleasure is usually down to experimentation. Pete wanted to give his girlfriend a good time.

Q Pete: How can I pleasure my kinky girlfriend?

I have a highly sexed girlfriend and we often talk about kinky things. I'd love to tie her up. I've never done this and would like to know how and where a woman likes to be restrained, and what enjoyment she might get from this.

A Being restrained in bondage-play heightens sexual tension for various reasons. Women often feel they can get into a bit of kinky role-play when tied up. They can protest to their partner they don't want anything 'bad' done to them, or that they're being 'taken against their will'. In a trusting sexual relationship, playing out such fantasies livens things up. Also the restrained partner can only really wriggle around, while the dominant partner stimulates them. This can amplify the sexual tension they feel. It can easily spill over into a fantasy game of a power struggle between 'master' and 'mistress'. If you want to try a little bondage-play without taking it too seriously, here are some suggestions to try partial restraint.

Steamy Sex Tip

Up the sexual tension by telling your partner in delicious detail what you're going to do to them...and then don't do it. For instance, saying you're going to stroke your partner's clitoris gently with a vibrator – then bringing it near to them – and then taking it away – will literally drive them crazy.

Time to get ready for bondage play

To get started with some bondage play, check out adult shops and internet sites (websites at the end of the book) that offer a wide range of restraints. But if you're a newcomer to bondage-play you can always experiment with items from around your home. But do be VERY careful with anything that wasn't made specially to be a sex toy, that it isn't potentially harmful. Use things like silky stockings or tights, a dressing gown sash or other sash, ribbon that you'd usually use for wrapping present, to tie bows with (remember bows, not knots.). You can even use a belt to buckle their wrists together as long as it's made of *soft* leather.

Or why not try some of the comfortable and ready-made 'bondage sheets' that have Velcro straps for the ankles and wrists. You can 'play safely' with these as there aren't any knots to get tangled up with. But some people are a bit put off by the 'manufactured' feel. Some couples would prefer to experience the spontaneity of grabbing whatever's handy to bind or be bound with.

Sex-periment with restraining these areas:

- Beginning with your hands, they can either be tied together or separately. There are many types of handcuffs/restraints available, as well as all sorts of ties, etc., to use. You can tie your lover's hands separately to a bed-head or even with long enough sashes to the legs of a bed or chair. You can bind their wrists together in front or behind them, but their comfort's all-important.

- Moving a bit further up – try tying their elbows together. You can pin the elbows back with a sash/belt – a man might find this a big turn on because it uplifts a woman's breasts if she's the one tied up. This might get uncomfortable quickly, but turn that into some of your sex-play. There's no rule that in one session you can only tie up one area. So tease your partner with a vibrator when their elbows are tied together, and then remove those ties and handcuff their hands together, and then tie them to the bed-head. And so on.

- Moving on to the legs, why not bind your lover's knees together. This will give you an unnaturally tight squeeze for penetrative sex when her knees are bound together, say, in spoons position.

This is definitely worth trying so you can experiment with different sensations.

❧ Ankles have been considered erotic since Victorian times, but they can be very ticklish like the knees – so use a firm grip when strapping your lover's ankles together. They'll have the sensation that they can't escape from the 'devilish and dominant' thing you're about to do to them. Tie their ankles together or separately to a bedstead or legs of a chair.

❧ Get seriously dominant and ask your partner to drop their inhibitions. Do this by doing bondage-play that literally puts their most intimate parts on display. For instance, ease your partner over the back of a comfy armchair so their head and shoulders rest in the seat, supported by extra cushions. Then tie their legs apart with their ankles bound to the chair legs. This completely exposes them and they'll be at your mercy for some oral pleasure or teasing with sex toys, etc. Not for the faint hearted.

❧ There are specialist shops for fetish-S&M-B&D furniture. If you wanted you could furnish an entire dungeon in your back bedroom. Specialist furniture varies from the extreme forms of medieval racks, stocks, punishment chairs, etc., to various types of wall and ceiling fixtures for 'stringing up' your lover. These are designed so that you don't cause your partner any damage when you use them properly. These items can completely expose your partner – not just for your voyeuristic pleasure, but also at an emotional level so you need to have lots of trust.

People get sexual thrills in all sorts of ways, and Janice wondered about getting kinky with blindfolds.

Q Janice: Blinded by passion?

My husband brought home a blindfold along with some sexy lingerie he bought for me. To be honest I'm not sure how erotic being blindfolded would be? We haven't got around to using it yet.

A He's recognised the eroticism of sensory deprivation, and it's amazing how you can heighten the sensitivity of your/your partner's skin by blindfolding them. Once you remove a sense (sight in this case), the other senses start to work overtime to compensate. This can have real benefits because it means your skin is more sensitive to touch. Blindfolds can be used in many ways, and for a couple that's lost the sensuality in their sex-play it's a good way of gently exploring their bodies and reconnecting at an intimate level. So go for it.

Steamy Sex Tips

Blindfolds are great for heightening erotic pleasures like 'feathering' – where your partner dribbles some massage oil down your body and then slowly traces the tip of a feather through it. Or during sexy 'ice play' where you lie back and your partner places an ice cube between their lips and traces the length of your body. They then alternate this by using their lips and tongue to warm up these areas.

Blindfolds definitely give an added edginess to sex-play. It can be incredibly erotic to listen to a fantasy scenario being described by your partner when you've got a blindfold on. It's easier to visualise the sexy scenes when your vision is taken away.

The big question for many is what to wear for this kind of sex-play. Charlotte felt the pressure to dress up for her partner.

Q Charlotte: Fancy dress sex?

My fiancé and I have been experimenting with a bit of tying up and spanking, and he wants me to dress up in some fetish-type clothes. I feel a bit foolish – any tips?

A

You don't have to go over the top when it comes to dressing for a bit of bondage bliss. It's likely you'll make a sexier impression if you choose one sexy piece of bondage gear rather than kitting yourself in head-to-toe fetish gear. The starting point is wearing the colours associated with domination like black and scarlet. Then you can add in your highest heels and sexy stockings, and you'll have created the right outfit.

Steamy Sex Tips

Go sexy shopping together where both of you (what's fair for her is fair for him.) try on different pieces of fetish gear. He might end up in a black leather studded man's thong. She might end up in a black PVC lace-up corset. Have fun trying things on in the shop – it'll put you in the mood to get home and get dressed up.

If you decide you enjoy bondage-play it's worthwhile for both of you to invest in some bondage gear. Each of you might have your own preferences and there may be some compromises to be made, but nowadays it's easy to get any type of gear – in leather, PVC, rubber – and loads of other stuff.

She might wear high-heeled, thigh-high boots or stilettos. And choose black stockings paired with something like a corset/basque *or* mini-skirt, so she doesn't feel completely over the top. He might want to get a genital bondage strap (there are loads of varieties.) or a slinky thong or one with leather and studs. These things can liven up your bondage-play.

Some people find it hard to understand that pain gives some people pleasure. Stella wondered about this.

Q Stella: How is pain pleasurable?

My boyfriend seems turned on by pain. He's asked me to whip or spank him and I just don't understand what pleasure he could get from this. I kind of understand the handcuff thing but not the pain thing.

A As I said earlier, sometimes the lines are blurred between different sexual practices like bondage and domination, and sadomasochism. In reality the definition isn't so important, but rather how you two feel about the sort of things you're willing to try – or not. Surrendering power allows some partners to relax and really enjoy the experience. And some relish a bit of pain as it enhances their sexual pleasure. Some people mean it when they joke, 'it hurts so good.' But others think that a bit of this type of fun just involves putting handcuffs on and being 'taken' while feeling restrained.

Talk about these things (remember the communication techniques from Chapter 4), and then you'll build the trust to feel comfortable doing them or not.

Steamy Sex Tip

One great technique to try when one partner wants to feel a bit of pain – or the thrill of potential pain – and the other doesn't want to inflict pain is this: tie that partner to a chair and the other can whip the floor around their feet. This way they are not inflicting pain but they're giving the partner who is tied up a bit of a thrill.

Insider info on spanking & whipping

You might just find when you play around with BDSM that you're willing to go a bit further. Also when it comes to spanking or whipping a partner – and you don't want to inflict pain – do it gently.

This might be a good point to mention that spanking and/or whipping can increase muscle tone. This in turn leaves it ready for further stimulation. Considering historical practices like self-flagellation (during religious festivities), remember that it would bring people to a state of emotional ecstasy – I'd guess with sexual undertones.

Also spanking and whipping increases the blood flow to the skin and can actually make a person more orgasmic. When you increase the blood flow to an area you also heighten sensations there, and this partly explains why some people love being spanked or whipped. Also the anticipation of getting spanked or whipped sends adrenaline coursing through our bodies, heightening the effect.

You can spank with so many different things, although investing in a padded 'paddle' from an adult shop is a good idea. But otherwise spank with your hand, or raid your kitchen for a big wooden spoon, or your bathroom for a hair brush. Some store-bought paddles have a fur-lined side for gentle action.

When it comes to whipping, there are a variety of 'vanilla' things that can serve as a whip like a dressing gown sash, to the 'hard-core' whips from a shop like thin leather whips guaranteed to inflict a sharp sting and probably draw blood.

Even if you want to stay away from bondage or S&M-play, you could deliver a quick smack or slap to the bottom or thighs during sex if you know your partner would enjoy it. But don't smack their bottom without sounding them out. Or try some 'pinching' as your partner reaches orgasm. This can play with their pain-pleasure threshold in a gentle way.

Don't forget that even mild and innocent forms of inflicting pain can be a big turn on, like your partner scratching their fingernails down the length of your back. Or ask them to gently tug your hair during sex.

A word of warning: exercise care and common sense at all times when doing any S&M. When your pain-pleasure threshold has been heightened and you're experiencing some jaw-juddering moments of sexual arousal, it's easy to stop erring on the side of common sense. For instance, never whip above your partner's waist, as you want to avoid your partner's eyes being accidentally hit. Also if you get into spanking and whipping you must change where you're delivering the 'action' on your partner's skin to avoid bruising and even permanent damage from repeated spankings/whippings – this damage can take the form of broken veins and mottled skin. So vary the places where you wield that spanking paddle. A professional 'top' (or 'dom' – the dominant party) knows this, but you may not. A 'bottom' (or 'sub' for submissive) is the partner who wants pain, humiliation, or both.

Sometimes it's the thrill of a verbal command that turns someone on. Roger wondered about his girlfriend's desire.

Q Roger: Sexy headmistress?

My girlfriend says that it turns her on to bark orders in the bedroom. I'm a little bit sceptical about why this would be?

A This doesn't surprise me, as many people are turned on just by hearing their lover bark some orders at them. Let's use the example of doing some role-play like in the film *The Secretary*. You can pretend that the 'boss' is unhappy with the 'secretary's' performance. He can bark an order to her to come and submit to him by bending over his desk. He then threatens punishment. Whether or not he actually spanks her bottom is one thing, but it's the sadistic manner in which he speaks to her that might turn her on. As long as you both know what the other finds a turn on and what they find utterly humiliating it will allow you to get the verbal tone just right.

Steamy Sex Tips

When it comes to verbal domination, agree the sorts of dirty words that are acceptable to you both. If the dominating partner lets loose with a hurricane of blue words, it might have the opposite effect and turn the submissive partner off. So have fun drawing up a 'naughty list' together.

≈

If the mood's right, you can drop in a bit of dirty talk – many people find it incredibly exciting. That's because we often don't use 'naughty words' in our sex life and it adds a bit of frisson.

Some find certain 'kinky' practices like anal sex quite shocking. Tammy was concerned by her husband's interest in this.

Q Tammy: Anal without pain?

My husband wants to try anal sex. Although I have no interest in doing it because I'm worried about the pain, part of me is simply curious. Is there a way to do it without any pain?

A Most people I've spoken to about their secret sexual desires wonder about certain 'forbidden fruit' – like anal sex. Traditionally anal sex has been viewed as forbidden despite being practised by various cultures down the ages, like the ancient Sumerians who had liberal views about sex and enjoyed practising both hetero- and homosexual anal sex. Anal sex gave pleasure to many couples long before other forms of birth control were practised. That said, a person must respect how their partner feels.

Steamy Sex Tips

Anal sex doesn't have to involve full penetration, and many find a little bit of 'anal-play' is pleasurable. Why not allow a partner to gently caress around your bottom, perineum and inner thigh as a starting point for sex-perimentation. Then a couple could move on to a little fingering around their/your anal opening. Practise safe sex, and don't allow contact between your fingers and anus – use sturdy clingfilm or a dental dam as a barrier.

After playing around in this way, you might allow your partner to slip a finger inside (they can put their finger in a condom) using loads of condom-friendly lubrication. Some couples might enjoy some anal 'rimming' – kissing and licking through a dental dam or clingfilm stimulating this sensitive area.

Anal sex

If you decide you want to try anal sex, follow these tips to make it as pain-free and pleasurable as possible. These tips are written as if a woman's going to be the 'receiver', but they apply equally to a man who wants anal stimulation from a vibrator, strap-on or a finger, or through gay sex:

- Begin by discussing this in a relaxed, caring and tactful way – listen to what the other says.

- Have an empty rectum before starting – either naturally or by using a suppository from a chemist if you're trying full penetration.

- Make sure you're both showered and your hands are clean before getting started. Even if you're going to slip your finger in a condom, any fumbling might mean you touch this delicate but germ-laden erogenous zone. You don't want to spread any germs between your hands and your anal area.

- Fingernails need to be trimmed and clean so they can't scratch or cause discomfort.

- Feeling relaxed definitely makes all the difference to anal penetration. This is true for the partner that'll be penetrated. If they are not relaxed, then it's impossible for their anal sphincter to relax. Don't forget that anal penetration is the exact opposite of what the sphincter and rectum were made for – relaxation is crucial.

- Loads of foreplay will help you both to feel relaxed and turned on.

- Anal penetration can be difficult, even with two partners who are keen, so always begin by indulging in a little 'anal-play'. Fingering with a well-lubricated condom on your finger is a great starting point. Insert one finger slowly and gently – simply leave it there without moving it. By leaving your finger to 'rest', it allows the outer anal sphincter to relax.

- Or you could indulge in a little anilingus, or 'rimming', as I've already mentioned. Place a dental dam between your tongue and the anus. Or if you want some penis-action, slip a condom on your penis and gently rub the tip of it around her anal area and perineum. This gentle action could relax and arouse her. Don't forget all of this requires a lot of trust.

- As the anal passage doesn't lubricate itself the way the vagina does, you must re-apply lots of water-based or condom-friendly lubricant throughout any anal pleasure. As well as using lashings of lube, ensure the condom is pre-lubricated.

- She can expel any trapped wind before penetration so she prevents any embarrassing noises during penetration. The technique for expelling any trapped wind before penetration is to get down on all fours and raise your hips in the air.

- People vary in the position they prefer during anal sex, but begin with a simple one like spoons. Or make sure she's well-supported by lots of pillows and try doggy style.

〰 One useful tip that might seem hard to understand, is for her to do the action necessary to gently expel wind as he starts penetration. This temporarily relaxes the sphincter, making the beginning of penetration easier.

〰 Despite their willingness and taking care, sometimes the partner receiving anal sex experiences pain or discomfort for a couple of days afterwards. Also, it may take a number of attempts to succeed at penetration.

Sex Doctor's Conclusions

We've now looked at many quirky and kinky sexual desires that I'm frequently asked about. People often ask me these things in the strictest confidence and expect me to be shocked because they assume they're the only person asking these questions. Let me reassure you they most definitely aren't the only ones asking. And even if you don't want to try these things you still might want to know about them.

The techniques I've recommended will help fulfil and satisfy these different desires but it's always crucial when crossing into quirky and kinky territory that you're considerate of your partner's feelings.

Many people won't even ask about their secret desires and keep them to themselves believing they're a bit too kinky. But it can enhance your sex life if you begin to talk about these. You never know, you might find your partner fantasises about the same things. There shouldn't be any embarrassment in sharing these things even if your partner isn't up for trying them out.

It's time to turn our attention to the bedrock of your sex life - your relationship and lifestyle. What happens in these definitely affects what happens in your sex life.

Chapter 7

Your relationship and lifestyle questions

19% of people say they'd feel sexier if slimmer

31% of people say a sense of humour puts them in the mood

So many things affect our relationship and how sexually satisfying it is. I've already highlighted some of the issues that affect how much sex you want with your partner – levels of sex drive, arousal and desire issues. Now I'd like to focus on other things that can come between you and a fantastic sex life.

Sandy raised a classic question that had an important impact on how sexually attractive she felt.

Q Sandy: How can I feel attractive again?

Since I had our second child ten months ago I've found it impossible to lose the last 7–8 pounds of excess weight. My husband doesn't seem to notice and still finds me desirable, but I feel so unattractive. I've always been trim and toned and now I feel like a lump. It's ruining our sex life.

A This is all about perception – here a wife perceives herself to be too large and unattractive, but her husband doesn't seem to notice. But just because they don't notice doesn't mean the partner who's put on weight doesn't feel completely unattractive. To begin with, a little self-discipline of your negative thinking goes a long way. Each time you think something like, 'I'm too fat to be sexy', immediately stop that thought and substitute it with a kinder one like, 'my partner's still attracted to me so I shouldn't worry.'

Next, think about boosting your metabolism with some fun exercise – it's not about losing weight but it is about feeling fitter and more vibrant. Think of something fun like going out dancing, bowling, tennis – anything you enjoy on your own or with your partner will help.

Always let your partner know when you're feeling sexually insecure. Together you can work on boosting your sexual confidence as well as your general confidence. Remind yourself daily of the best qualities you have outside of the bedroom.

Steamy Sex Tips

To boost your body confidence, get some sexy new lingerie and slip into it, wear it around and enjoy feeling good in it. Once you're feeling body-confident again go for some outrageous flirting. Phone or text your partner and tell them you've slipped into something really sexy. Ask them to guess what you're doing and where you're touching yourself. Have fun with phone-sex to give you the confidence to have some real fun when they get home.

One massive confidence booster is to play out a sexual fantasy where you are a desirable film star and your partner's your number one fan. Have fun with sex-chat about how your fan can't get enough of you and would do anything to please you in bed.

Boredom in the bedroom

Unfortunately another classic bedroom dilemma for long-term couples is boredom in the bedroom. Gerry loved his wife, but felt bored.

Q Gerry: Keeping things fresh

I love my wife to bits but despite that I find myself bored with our bedroom routine. Please help before this becomes a problem between us.

A Boredom in the bedroom is the responsibility of *both* people. It's easy to point the finger at the partner who, say, might be shyer about sex-perimenting or is satisfied with the same sex every time. In such cases it's the other partner's responsibility to lead the way and seduce them into trying new things. What's crucial is to understand why that person seems happy with the same old sex. Is it shyness or inhibition? Is it that they're easier to please? Is it they just don't know what to try?

Once you understand why she hasn't wanted to try new things, you can start introducing something pleasurable to tempt her with. You can do this easily by trying new things outside the bedroom like listening to new music, visiting different restaurants, doing something you have never done before as a couple.

Steamy Sex Tips

One fantastic way to stimulate a partner's desire to try new things is during foreplay. When you're cuddling up start stroking their favourite erogenous zone. But only stroke it to the point of teasing them rather than satisfying them. As their desire gets more and more heightened, start describing the sort of thing you'd like to try – like getting them into a new and exciting sex position. You can say something like, 'I've always wanted to take you from behind because then I could reach around and fondle your breasts as I gently thrust back and forth inside you.' I think you get the picture – you make sex-perimenting sound so hot that they say, 'Let's try it.'

≈

Try a fun sex game that takes the pressure off both of you when you're trying to introduce new things. Play a simple game of sexy dice – on a piece of paper, mark down what each number on the dice represents. For instance, rolling a '1' = kissing her breasts. Rolling a '2' = you get to choose a new position. Rolling a '3' = five minutes of sensual massage wherever you want it. Rolling a '4' = 10 minutes of oral pleasure. Rolling a '5' = using a sex toy, etc. Using the dice to select new things for you to try makes it fun and less daunting.

≈

Another great tip is to take a sex guide like this – sit down together, and randomly open to a page, and together choose something to try out. Again this puts your sex life in the hands of fate, taking the responsibility away from you. With some subtle lighting and mood music on, this is an easy way to discover some new sex-play.

≈

Finally, simply changing the room you normally have sex in, say, from the bedroom into a comfy corner of the sitting room, can make all the difference and make sex feel fresh.

Let's get sex-perimental: pressure in the bedroom

Some of the issues that have a real impact on a sexual relationship are very complicated. Nancy felt under pressure from her long-term partner to try something she wasn't so sure of.

Q Nancy: Three's company...?

I've been with my boyfriend for five years, we've lived together for three, and I see it as a long-term thing. The only problem is he's always wanted to try a threesome and I feel intimidated by this. I don't want what we have spoiled by something that could backfire.

A

Understandably, when one partner wants to introduce something pretty intense, like trying a threesome, it can be threatening and daunting. This applies to threesomes, swinging, visiting fetish clubs, etc. So, as when I mentioned anal sex in the last chapter, no one should feel pressured into doing something they don't want to do.

Although as a fantasy threesomes can be highly erotic, it takes a sexually confident couple to enjoy them without them threatening their relationship. Often the reality is very different from the fantasy – and they can be disappointing – so this is something to think about.

Steamy Sex Tip

Enjoy some fantasy-play around threesomes. You might choose to watch a porn DVD that's about threesomes or group sex. Or you can get involved in super-detailed and erotic fantasy chat of exactly what you'd do if you had a threesome. I've known plenty of couples satisfied with such fantasy chat. One fantasy that can serve this purpose is the man pretending he's a 'company director' and he's 'hired' his partner as his 'PA'. Not only does she have to satisfy his demanding sexual desires, but she also has to take part in a threesome with another colleague. There are tons of fantasy possibilities in discussing such fantasies, which will turn you both on without being threatening.

Ground rules for three-way sex

It's crucial to your relationship to set some ground rules – that you both agree on – if you decide to try something like three-way sex, to make sure the threesome doesn't get out of hand. Classic ground rules include:

((Selecting a third party who isn't close to either of you. It's unwise to involve a friend. Many couples who want to try this go to events catering to this, or find a third person from a contact magazine/website.

((Agree exactly what sexual behaviour is acceptable or not. For instance, some couples decide that kissing on the lips is too intimate. Yup, I know, it doesn't seem to make sense because they're fine about full sex not being too intimate. But who am I to judge?

((Negotiate what potential contact outside of your sexual arrangement is allowed or not. To 'protect' their relationship, most couples don't allow seeing the third-party apart from when they're all together as a threesome.

((Be tactful with your partner's feelings about what you enjoyed in the threesome. Saying that it was the 'best sex' you ever had – and that the third party is really 'hot' – isn't particularly tactful.

Many couples are affected by whether one or the other is more experimental when it comes to their sex life. Penny wished her husband could be more experimental.

Q Penny: The elusive G spot

My husband and I have a very good relationship although I worry that things have got stale in the bedroom, and I feel I'd love to experiment but he isn't bothered about that. For instance, I feel like

I'm the only woman in the world who hasn't even tried to find her G spot with her husband.

A I'm glad that the G spot has been raised – researchers still can't agree whether or not it exists, but you can have fun trying to find it. I think it's a fantastic way for couples to sex-periment a little by looking for it. I often find that when you start 'small' then you get big results. A partner that's been a bit lazy or worried about experimenting realises it's not so hard to have a little fun.

As in the earlier chapter on communication – it's the way you introduce things that can make it an issue or fun. The next time you're cuddling-up say something like, 'I sometimes get extra sensations during sex and I wonder if you're stimulating my G spot?' That'll get him interested.

Your G spot (if you're sensitive in this area) is located up inside your vagina on the front wall (tummy-button side) of your vagina. It should feel like a spongy mass of tissue about the size of a 10-pence coin. When stimulated you get distinct sensations. Whether you actually have a G spot or just feel different sensations in this area doesn't matter – relax and enjoy.

 Steamy Sex Tips

Have your partner use lots of luscious lubricant while he's exploring your G 'zone', as I like to call it (why limit it to a single spot when you're trying to find it?). He can rub lots on his penis or on your vagina – with sensual strokes. Then when he enters, you tell him in the sexiest possible way exactly what his different moves feel like. He can thrust in and out and then gently circle with his hips – and you can let him know if it feels anything from 'heavenly' to 'I can hardly feel it'.

≈

If he's using his fingers to locate your G zone, ask him to gently circle it with the tip of his finger. He can experiment with stroking it, sliding his finger back and forth over it and even gently 'tapping' it too.

Have fun with G-spot vibrators that have a convenient bend in them for stimulating the 'front' wall of her vagina in the hopes of tickling the elusive spot. Some of these are on a 'wand' – with a vibrator on the end for direct G-spot stimulation – and others are thicker. Women who've tried them say they can be fantastic. Get daring and let him vibrate you from behind as you crouch on your hands and knees on the bed. Do this in some sexy lingerie.

G-spot position

When you're on the G zone 'search', there are a couple of sex positions that are best for stimulating it. One of the best positions for getting G-spot action is 'girls on top'. Begin by lying on him body-against-body, you're on top but then you raise yourself up to a 'sitting' position. This gives the added bonus of allowing him full access to your breasts. Why not smooth lots of lovely lubricant across them, and allow him to swirl it all over you.

While in this sitting-on-top position try doing a few circular, grinding motions stimulating all sides of your vagina including the front wall where your G spot is (again, if it exists). This feels incredibly erotic – G spot or not.

You can also try good old spoons position. This is the perfect, comfy position for a slow Sunday-morning sex session, but it also stimulates many sensitive spots inside you, including the G spot. He can try varying the depth and motion of his penetration while you try varying your leg position. He can take charge and lift your upper leg, at your thigh, to increase or decrease tension on his penis. For instance, if you're both lying on your right sides this'll be your left thigh. By slipping his hand under your thigh and supporting it, he can vary the area inside you that he touches with his thrusting. Let him know when he hits the front wall of your vagina and then he can swivel his hips in small circular motions to massage your G spot.

Try doggy style too, as that gives him perfect access to your G zone. Again ask him to vary his thrusting – some back and forth, to around and around – maximising the pleasure deep inside you.

Sex toy oh-oh-heaven

Often partners have different opinions on what's 'right' and 'wrong' when it comes to their relationship generally, and specifically when experimenting in their sex life as Alistair found.

Q Alistair: Sex toy story

Please help, my partner seems to think that sex toys are only for sex maniacs. I think there's nothing wrong with them and I'd like to convince her of this. She is much more conservative than I am and this does affect our relationship, but it's our sex life I think could be more adventurous.

A I mentioned earlier about the benefit of choosing porn together, and it's the same with sex toys – suggest going on a little adult shopping spree. Most of the adult shops on the high street are inviting, brightly lit and incredibly non-threatening, so even the most conservative partner might be tempted along. Make an evening of it – first a little sexy shopping, dinner and then home to try out your latest purchases.

It's far better to choose something together then to spring a sex toy on a partner that might be a little bit inhibited. Also avoid the large, lurid-coloured ones that can be intimidating and a turn off.

Steamy Sex Tip

Why not try the 'tongue joy' vibrator – slip it on your tongue and vibrate around your partner's different erogenous zones? This can work while you give her oral sex, or even just by kissing behind her ears where it can vibrate that much-neglected erogenous zone. Why not give him extra pleasure in spoons position – she can slip her hands between their legs to tickle his perineum and testicles with a vibrator. He'll love it.

The toy box

Don't forget, men are sometimes intimidated by the larger vibrators that make them feel inadequate. And as with Alistair's wife many women feel inhibited about trying sex toys.

With that in mind there's a huge variety of sex toys available in high street adult shops or online. Here are some of the most popular ones to try beginning with those that don't require batteries:

- Persian love beads – these come on a string that's inserted into the vagina or anally. These beads move around as the user moves giving her/him lots of erotic sensations. Have fun by telling your partner you've popped them in and the gentle teasing sensations are putting you in the mood for sex later on.

- Take things a step further – she can insert the love beads anally and then have sex with her partner for double the pleasure. For an advanced technique, he can gently pull the beads out one at a time during her orgasm to enhance it. And she can do the same to him if he wears them during sex to stimulate his prostate gland. There are new 'soft' pliable beads available for a gentler experience.

- Oriental love balls/eggs – these come as a pair and are made for vaginal stimulation. As she moves around they move around giving her nice sensations. Be a bit daring and ask your partner to insert them for you. And play a secret game where you both know they're in your vagina – stimulating you – as you go about errands during the day.

❀ Anal/'butt' plugs – although originally created for gay pleasure, butt plugs are enjoyed by some women and also straight men. Imagine the shape of a mini-lava lamp that holds itself in place in the rectum by the slightly bulbous end. Use lots of lubrication (same as with the love beads above), as the anal passage does not lubricate itself. Plugs come in a range of sizes giving different sensations before sex, during foreplay and during penetration (for a woman).

❀ Dildos – these are non-vibrating penis-shaped sex toys. Some couples prefer these because the buzzing of a battery operated vibrator is distracting – even with the new 'quiet' ones. These are manipulated by your hand to stimulate the vagina or anus by moving it in and out, and around, in circular motions.

❀ The 'Saturn Crystal Wand' – this dildo is gorgeous looking with some lovely lumps and bumps for extra stimulation. This'll reach your G spot.

❀ Strap-on dildos – 30% of these are bought by straight couples rather than lesbians. He can live out all sorts of fantasies while being penetrated by her. You need to practise with strap-ons, so don't give up with your first attempt. Always start slowly (isn't this true of most sex play?) with gentle thrusts. It's crucial that a strap-on fits well or you'll lose the pleasurable side of the experience.

❀ Penile shaft sleeves – a fun little item for extra stimulation. These are flexible, soft 'sleeves' that he can put on his finger or the shaft of the penis for extra stimulation of her clitoris, labia and vagina. There are a variety of styles with different ridges and 'knobbles' to experiment with. Use lubricant on these to increase her pleasure. She can also use a sleeve over two fingers when manually stimulating him. Don't forget he'll love new sensations as much as she does. Also try changing the sensation of your vibrator by slipping a 'sleeve' on it.

When it comes to battery-operated toys, a lot of finesse goes into contemporary ones, using natural colours and often artistic shapes. Not only can you both have fun with vibrators but they're ideal for masturbation (even mutual masturbation.) and I strongly advise women that have difficulty reaching orgasm to try using a vibrator. Sex therapists recommend experimenting with vibrators in comfortable surroundings when feeling relaxed. This will definitely help you get to know your own sexual responses.

- Fingertip vibrators – these small but perfectly formed toys can be used to vibrate her clitoral region. But don't stop there, as they feel fabulous on the nipples, the perineum and other erogenous zones. Try the 'Zing Finger' that's guaranteed to give you a zing.

- Clitoral ticklers – these can come attached to regular vibrators or on their own and have little attachments for added pleasure. Some have little 'knobbles' of feather-like ticklers that vibrate gently over her clitoris.

- 'G-spot Aqua Vibe' – guaranteed to give you bath-time bliss as it's waterproof. It's got a 'come over here' style, 'crooked' finger design with multi-speed settings so that you can choose very subtle to more powerful vibrations.

- 'Vibrating Rock Chick' – an ingenious shape that stimulates both the G spot and her clitoral region simultaneously. The drawback is that the vibrations are subtle so it might not work for a woman who likes strong vibrations.

- The 'Jessica Rabbit', or 'Pearl Rabbit' – this rather strange looking but very successful vibrator is super popular. The main vibrator penetrates the vagina while the little ears of the 'rabbit' vibrate either side of her clitoris.

- The 'Micro Rabbit Stretch Cock Ring' – a truly fun sex toy for couples. It's waterproof and made of flexible silicone with a multi-speed clitoris-tickling 'rabbit'.

- Multiple vibrators – there are now some weird and wonderful vibrators that have anal, vaginal and clitoral stimulating heads in one toy. For the skilled lover these give a complete experience. The Three-way Rabbit is a popular version of the multiple vibrator that tickles her clitoris and stimulates her vagina and also her anal area. To be honest it looks pretty hideous – like a lot of the rabbit toys – but it hits the spot.

Touch me, feel me

Sometimes all a person needs is some loving touch from their partner and that'd be the icing on the cake for them. The power of touch can't be underestimated, and as you know I've already discussed various touching techniques in Chapter 5. Linda felt like she was drifting away from her husband because of the lack of touch between them.

Q Linda: Sensual massage

I love my husband very much but I feel we're drifting apart because I crave his attention in sensual and loving ways. When it comes to foreplay he touches me and gets me aroused, but what I'd love is some sensual massage – and feeling like I had his complete attention. Is that too much to ask?

A Touch is terribly important to intimacy, and sensual massage can be an important part of that. This is because loving, physical contact between two people leads to the production of oxytocin

– the emotional bonding hormone. Oxytocin helps to strengthen the bond between you, and leads to more touching – so it enhances a wonderful cycle of more and more touch. When it comes to two people – often with two very different sets of needs – sometimes only one feels the need for a lot of touch. Using the communication techniques from Chapter 4 should help you get the physical contact you desire.

It might be the case you can encourage your partner to give you a massage by seizing the moment when they touch you sensually even in passing. At that moment tell them how wonderful it feels and ask for more of that exact stroke. Or it might work to offer to massage them in return for them massaging you. If you say it in a flirty and fun way, rather than a critical way, it works.

Sometimes a person just wants the closeness of a massage. And you're wrong if you think massage and sex are intrinsically linked. However, when your partner is tenderly massaging you – as long as it's pleasurable to you – it might stimulate sexy feelings. Those feelings can either be acted upon – and the massage leads to full sex – or they can simply be enjoyed.

I don't believe sensual massage should always lead to full sex. As that puts enormous pressure on a couple to always feel they have to take sensual touching to full sex. A couple's less likely to enjoy a massage if there's overriding pressure that it has to lead 'somewhere'.

So, let your partner know if you're happy to relax and enjoy a massage, without it having to go somewhere. If it does, that's great but not necessary.

Steamy Sex Tip

Why not try a very sensual type of massage – the 'Oriental hair massage'. Your partner lies naked on the bed as you crouch over them and swish your hair back and forth across their chest, hips and thighs. Men can do this to their partners despite having short hair - they can swirl it around her breasts and nipples, down her abdomen and across her hips and pubic mound - a very simple way to take her to heaven. And you can develop it into the 'Oriental body massage; where you glide your topless chest over their topless chest and your hips over their hips.

≈

To make your massage a super hot experience, turn it into a fantasy chat. Suggest to your partner that you'd like him to pretend he's a handsome hotel porter who has come in - and found you getting out of the shower. He was going to 'restock the room with fresh towels' but now he's going to 'service' all your needs.

Something that shouldn't be forgotten is that what feels good to one person may not feel good to another. Nathan didn't like the way his girlfriend massaged him.

Q Nathan: I need a gentler touch

How do I break it to my girlfriend when she's giving me a massage that she's doing it wrong? I don't like the way she does it – far too hard – but she's really into it and I don't want to upset her.

A The best way to encourage a massage/touch that you enjoy is to wait for the moment when a heavy-handed partner actually does something that even *begins* to feel right. The moment they lighten or change their touch to something that feels good, tell them immediately how wonderful it feels. Ask them to repeat it. By building their confidence that they're doing something right, you can encourage more of that type of caressing.

If they then go back to the massage technique that doesn't feel good, rather than criticise them you can say something simple like, 'I loved what you were doing, can you please do more of that?' Guide their hands back to that place or describe what they were doing well.

If it's a case of them hurting you or turning you off with their massage, there's nothing wrong with you tactfully, but directly, saying that it doesn't feel particularly good. Help them by making suggestions as to what you enjoy.

When your relationship gets in the way of sex

As I mentioned in Chapter 1, the state of your relationship affects your sex life in so many ways. Michelle got in touch about a classic way this can happen.

Q **Michelle: Make-up sex**

My boyfriend and I have a tumultuous relationship with lots of arguing and then making up. I suspect he loves the make-up sex, but I find my heart is less and less in it. I'd rather get along with him than have that passionate make-up sex.

A It's obvious to me that the excitement of make-up sex can lose that power over time, and actually can damage your relationship further, as Michelle's finding. Always begin by identifying the 'hotspots' that sets off your arguing. It could be financial issues, who does what around your home, arguing over tidying up or the lack of it, visiting each other's families, etc., the list is endless for an individual couple's 'hotspots'.

Once identified, sit down and work out some solutions. Tell your partner how much you'd love to have a quieter life with them. Together you two can brainstorm how to get rid of these 'hotspots'.

If you find you can't get on top of arguments and they're eating away at your relationship (and sex life) then find out about married/relationship guidance services like Relate.

Steamy Sex Tip

Once things are calmer, you can still generate passionate sex. Put on some pulsating music, touch and caress with abandon, tease them and strip for them. Jump in the shower together, try a new position in it ('strip search' mentioned earlier in the book is perfect), and generally let your passion flow during sex. Far better than flowing in rows.

It's the little things that keeps things hot

You may not experience many rows and difficulties in your relationship. And things might generally be ticking over nicely for you as a couple. Often when things are pretty good, one or other of the partners don't want to make a big deal out of trying to spice things up – even if they'd like to. So to take the stress out of trying new things, remember it can be the little things that make all the difference, as I told Karen.

Q Karen: Spicing it up

I'm very satisfied with my long-term partner – and I feel quite selfish asking about spicing things up – but I wonder if there are little ways we could inject some excitement so that it doesn't feel contrived.

A There are many, many little ways to spice things up. To begin with, most couples get stuck having sex at a certain time of day – usually mornings or evenings. Simply vary that for starters. Next most common is that people have sex on the same day of the week, for example always on a Sunday morning. Vary the day of the week you have sex too.

Now we can move on to location – if you always have sex in the bedroom it gets boring. You can have sex practically anywhere as long as you've got a cushion or two to pad anything like your knees or bottom. Sometimes this sort of 'spontaneity' actually needs planning. So have a think about places you could make love. At home try the bathroom counter, kitchen table, kneeling against the sofa, on the carpet, in an easy chair, across the stairs... Outside gets a bit risky but you can, say, get things started by touching-up your partner while sitting in a restaurant, ostensibly looking at the menus. Be creative and you'll be dying to try something new.

Steamy Sex Tips

Turning food into a bit of rude-food is fun. Mix up a couple of cocktails, and with the straw allow some drops to cascade down her breasts for him to lick off. Hand-feed each other anything creamy like chocolate mousse, cream pie, cakes or most desserts – and gently kiss away any drops that miss your mouth. Have a mini-feast in bed by candlelight and choose foods you can feed each other easily.

Don't forget ice is nice. Take an ice cube from your drink, put it between your lips and trace it right down your partner's body. Then retrace that cool path with your lips and tongue without the ice cube. Alternate these sensations with the ice, and then without the ice.

Make a monthly date to try new techniques and look through this book for suggestions. Remember the old saying: use it or lose it – and this counts for your sensual/sexual creativity – if you don't use your imagination a little then it's easy to lose altogether.

Make a note in your diary to make little efforts – even sending a sexy text during the day or leaving them a loving note in their paperwork can put a spring in their step. Never forget the power of your voice – a flirty phone call during the day describing what you'd like to do to them that evening will make it hard for them to concentrate on work that afternoon.

Final words

I hope I've given you lots of ideas for you to try. Through the very words of the people I hear from, and the questions they want answers to, I hope you've discovered lots about how to improve your sexual relationship. Let me finish on my 'Three Cs of Successful Sex': confidence, communication and creativity.

If you develop the *confidence* (hopefully helped by my suggestions to build confidence) to believe that you're worthy of a great sex life – and a more intimate relationship – then you're much more likely to get it. If you use the *communication* skills I've given you – to express what you'd like in the bedroom and find out what your partner would like – sexual satisfaction is probably guaranteed. And finally with just a bit of *creativity* you can make things much hotter and more exciting. Simply by varying and altering how you touch, caress, kiss and sex-periment with your partner with positions and techniques, you're much more likely to both be satisfied.

Happy loving, Dr Pam X

Useful websites

Here is a selection of the many adult websites out there. Most of these are straightforward sites selling a range of sex toys and products, though I have added notes for those that offer information, advice or other services. **It is your responsibility to ensure that at the time of use any website is secure.**

Please note that all websites are prefixed with www.

a
adameve.com
agentprovocateur.com
angelicweapons.co.uk
annsummers.com
athenafem.co.uk– for pelvic muscle exercises

b
bedroompleasures.co.uk
blissbox.com
blushingbuyer.co.uk

c
cherrybliss.com
cliterati.co.uk
coco-de-mer.co.uk
condomania.co.uk
couplebox.com – software to store your private pictures securely
curiosa.co.uk – for erotica

d
doublydiscreet.com
dreamgirldirect.co.uk

e
elegantlywaisted.co.uk
emotionalbliss.com
erotica-readers.co.uk
eroticprints.org
eternalspirits.com

f
femininezone.com– for information and advice
femmefun.com
fetteredpleasures.com
flirtyordirty.co.uk

g
getmepleasure.co.uk
glamorousamorous.com
goodvibes.com

h
highestheaven.co.uk
hunkystrippers.com

i
idlube.co.uk – specialises in lubricants

l
lovehoney.co.uk

m
male101.com – about male sexuality
mencorp.com – for strippers
menforaloccasions.com – for escorts

mr-s-leather-fetters.com
myla.com

n
natural-contours.com
no-angel.com

p
passion8.com – erotica
pelvictoner.co.uk
pillowtalk.co.uk

s
sda.uk.net – the sexual dysfunction association
serpentstail.com – for hot reading
sexchanpionships.com – a sex game to play online
sexplained.com – for information on stis, etc.
sexshop365.co.uk
sextoys.co.uk
sh-womenstore.com
shesaidboutique.com
skintwo.com
slap.dat.co.uk – a butt-slapping fun site
slashfic.co.uk – your favourite fictional charcaters are given hot scenes

t
takemetobed.co.uk – for erotica and porn
thesexystore.co.uk

w
whysleep.co.uk
wickedlywildwomen.com
willyworries.com